PUF

SLAVES

You are an adventurer famed throughout Allansia. You find yourself in the city of Kallamehr at a time of crisis. The city is threatened by invasion from the east – and the army is absent! Lady Carolina of Kallamehr summons you to her presence: it is up to YOU to save the city. You do not hesitate to offer your services, but what can you do? What plan is best? Time is not on your side – and there are dangers more concrete than time to overcome as well!

Two dice, a pencil and an eraser are all you need to embark on this thrilling adventure, which is complete with its elaborate combat system and a score-sheet to record your gains and losses.

Many dangers lie ahead and your success is by no means certain. YOU decide which routes to follow, which dangers to risk and which adversaries to fight!

Fighting Fantasy Gamebooks

1. THE WARLOCK OF FIRETOP MOUNTAIN
2. THE CITADEL OF CHAOS
3. THE FOREST OF DOOM
4. STARSHIP TRAVELLER
5. CITY OF THIEVES
6. DEATHTRAP DUNGEON
7. ISLAND OF THE LIZARD KING
8. SCORPION SWAMP
9. CAVERNS OF THE SNOW WITCH
10. HOUSE OF HELL
11. TALISMAN OF DEATH
12. SPACE ASSASSIN
13. FREEWAY FIGHTER
14. TEMPLE OF TERROR
15. THE RINGS OF KETHER
16. SEAS OF BLOOD
17. APPOINTMENT WITH F.E.A.R.
18. REBEL PLANET
19. DEMONS OF THE DEEP
20. SWORD OF THE SAMURAI
21. TRIAL OF CHAMPIONS
22. ROBOT COMMANDO
23. MASKS OF MAYHEM
24. CREATURE OF HAVOC
25. BENEATH NIGHTMARE CASTLE
26. CRYPT OF THE SORCERER
27. STAR STRIDER
28. PHANTOMS OF FEAR
29. MIDNIGHT ROGUE
30. CHASMS OF MALICE
31. BATTLEBLADE WARRIOR

Steve Jackson's SORCERY!
1. The Shamutanti Hills
2. Kharé – Cityport of Traps
3. The Seven Serpents
4. The Crown of Kings

FIGHTING FANTASY – The Role-playing Game
THE RIDDLING REAVER
OUT OF THE PIT – Fighting Fantasy Monsters
TITAN – The Fighting Fantasy World

Steve Jackson and Ian Livingstone
present:

SLAVES OF THE ABYSS

by Paul Mason and Steve Williams

Illustrated by Bob Harvey

PUFFIN BOOKS

For Gail and P.S.

PUFFIN BOOKS

Published by the Penguin Group
27 Wrights Lane, London W8 5TZ, England
Viking Penguin Inc., 40 West 23rd Street, New York, New York 10010, USA
Penguin Books Australia Ltd, Ringwood, Victoria, Australia
Penguin Books Canada Ltd, 2801 John Street, Markham, Ontario, Canada L3R 1B4
Penguin Books (NZ) Ltd, 182–190 Wairau Road, Auckland 10, New Zealand

Penguin Books Ltd, Registered Offices: Harmondsworth, Middlesex, England

First published 1988
Reprinted 1988

Printed and bound in Great Britain by
Cox & Wyman Ltd, Reading
Filmset in 11/13pt Palatino by
Rowland Phototypesetting Ltd,
Bury St Edmunds, Suffolk

CONTENTS

INTRODUCTION

Your Character

In this book you are a famous adventurer in the lands of Allansia, the veteran of many battles and the doer of many fine deeds. You have in your possession a finely wrought sword of Fangthane steel and your sturdy backpack. Before embarking on this, your latest adventure, you must first determine your strengths and weaknesses.

You use dice to determine your initial SKILL and STAMINA scores. On pages 16–17 there is an *Adventure Sheet* on which you may record the details of your adventure. There you will find boxes for recording your SKILL and STAMINA scores.

You are unlikely to complete this adventure successfully at the first attempt, so you are advised either to record your scores on the *Adventure Sheet* in pencil or to make photocopies of the page for use in future attempts.

Skill, Stamina and Luck

Roll one die. Add 6 to this number and enter the total in the SKILL box on the *Adventure Sheet*.

Roll two dice. Add 12 to the number rolled and enter the total in the STAMINA box.

There is also a LUCK box. Roll one die, add 6 to this number and enter the total in the LUCK box.

For reasons that will be explained below, SKILL, STAMINA and LUCK scores change constantly during an adventure. You must keep an accurate record of these scores, and for this reason you are advised either to write small in the boxes or to keep an eraser handy. But never rub out your *Initial* scores. Although you may be awarded additional SKILL, STAMINA and LUCK points, these totals may never exceed your *Initial* scores, except on very rare occasions when you will be instructed in a particular paragraph.

Your SKILL score reflects your swordsmanship and general fighting expertise; the higher the better. Your STAMINA score reflects your general constitution, your will to survive, your determination and overall fitness; the higher your STAMINA score, the longer you will be able to survive. If your STAMINA score drops to zero, stop reading, close the book and then start again from the beginning. Your LUCK score indicates how naturally lucky a person you are. Luck – and magic – are facts of life in the fantasy kingdom you are about to explore.

Combat

You will often come across paragraphs in the book where you are instructed to fight a creature of some sort. An option to flee may be given, but if not – or if you choose to attack the creature anyway – you must resolve the battle as described below.

First record your opponent's SKILL and STAMINA scores in the first empty Monster Encounter Box on your *Adventure Sheet*. The scores for every potential adversary are given each time you have an encounter. The sequence for combat is then:

1. Roll two dice for the opponent. Add its SKILL score. This total is the opponent's Attack Strength.
2. Roll two dice for yourself. Add the number rolled to your current SKILL score. This total is your Attack Strength.
3. If your Attack Strength is higher than that of the opponent, you have wounded it: proceed to step 4. If your opponent's Attack Strength is higher than yours, it has wounded you: proceed to step 5. If both Attack Strength totals are the same, you have avoided each other's blows – start the next Attack Round from step 1, above.
4. You have wounded the creature, so subtract 2 points from its STAMINA score. (You may use your LUCK here to do additional damage – see below.)
5. The creature has wounded you, so subtract 2 points from your own STAMINA score. (Again you may use LUCK at this stage – see below.)
6. Make the appropriate adjustments either to the opponent's or to your own STAMINA score (and to your LUCK score if you used LUCK – see below).

7. Begin the next Attack Round by returning to your current SKILL score and repeating steps 1–6. This sequence continues until the STAMINA score of either you or your adversary has been reduced to zero (death).

Escaping

In some paragraphs you will be given the option of running away from a battle should things be going badly for you. However, if you do run away, your opponent automatically gets in one wound on you (deduct 2 STAMINA points) as you flee – such is the price of cowardice. (Note that you may use LUCK to minimize this wound in the normal way – see below.) You may *Escape* only if that option is specifically given to you in the paragraph.

Fighting More Than One Opponent

If you come across more than one possible adversary in an encounter, the instructions in that paragraph will tell you how to handle the battle. Sometimes you will treat them as a single opponent; sometimes you will have to fight each in turn.

Instant Death

You are a mighty warrior, with a blade of finest Fangthane steel. Whenever you roll a double 6 in battle you have scored a *killing blow* on your opponent. The battle ends straight away, and you are the victor!

You may inflict *killing blows* on your opponents only if you are using your sword. If you ever lose the sword, you will forfeit this special ability.

Luck

At various times during your adventure, either in battle or when you find yourself in a situation in which you could be either lucky or unlucky (on each occasion you are invited to *Test your Luck* in the relevant paragraph), you have to call on your LUCK to make the outcome more favourable. But beware! Using LUCK is a risky business, and if you are *un*lucky, the results could be disastrous.

The procedure for *Testing your Luck* is as follows: roll two dice. If the number rolled is *equal to or less than* your current LUCK score, you have been Lucky and the result will go in your favour. If the number rolled is *higher than* your current LUCK score, you have been Unlucky and you will be penalized.

Each time you *Test your Luck*, you must subtract 1 point from your current LUCK score. You will soon come to realize that the more you rely on your LUCK, the more risky this will become.

Using Luck in Battles

In certain paragraphs you will be told to *Test your Luck* and will then discover the consequences of being Lucky or Unlucky. However, you always have the option of using your LUCK in battle, either to inflict a more serious wound on an opponent you have just wounded, or to reduce the effects of a wound the opponent has just inflicted on you.

If you have just won an Attack Round, you may *Test your Luck* as described above. If you are Lucky, you have inflicted a severe wound on your opponent and may subtract an extra 2 points from the creature's STAMINA score. However, if you are Unlucky, the wound was a mere graze and you must restore 1 point to its STAMINA (i.e. instead of scoring the normal 2 points of damage, you have now scored only 1).

If you have just lost an Attack Round and been wounded, you may *Test your Luck* to try to lessen the wound. If you are Lucky, you have managed to avoid the full impact of the blow. Restore 1 point of STAMINA (so that, instead of doing 2 points of damage, it has done only 1). If you are Unlucky, you have had to take a more serious blow. Subtract 1 *extra* STAMINA point.

Remember: you must subtract 1 point from your LUCK score every time you *Test your Luck*.

Restoring Skill, Stamina and Luck

Skill

Your SKILL score will not change much during your adventure. Occasionally, a paragraph may give the instruction to increase or decrease your SKILL score. A special weapon may also increase your SKILL; but remember that only one weapon can be used at a time! You cannot claim two SKILL bonuses for carrying two magic swords.

Stamina and Provisions

Your STAMINA score will change a lot during your adventure as you fight monsters and undertake arduous tasks. As you near your goal, your STAMINA level may become dangerously low and battles may be particularly risky, so be careful!

Your backpack contains enough Provisions for five meals. You may rest and eat at any time except when engaged in a battle. Eating a meal restores up to 4 STAMINA points. When you eat a meal, add up to 4 points to your STAMINA score and deduct one of your Provisions. A separate Provisions Remaining Box is provided on the *Adventure Sheet* for this purpose. Remember that you have a long way to go, so use your Provisions wisely!

Remember also that your STAMINA score may never exceed its *Initial* value.

Luck

Additions to your LUCK score are awarded during the adventure when you have been particularly lucky; details of when this occurs are given in the relevant paragraphs. Remember: as with STAMINA, your LUCK score may never exceed its *Initial* value.

Equipment

You will start your adventure with a bare minimum of equipment, but you will probably acquire other items during your travels. You are armed with a fine steel sword which has carried you through countless fights, and you are dressed in your battered leather armour. You have 5 Gold Pieces left from your last adventure, and a backpack to hold your Provisions and any treasures you may come across.

Keeping Track of Time

The adventure which lies ahead of you is a race against time. A grave threat hangs over Kallamehr, and only by quick and resourceful action will you be able to defeat it.

As you make your choices, from time to time you will find instructions to 'tick off a time box'. Whenever you come upon one of these, you should make a pencil mark in the first available empty box on the *Time Sheet* provided on the inside front cover. Start with the box at the top left, and move from left to right and from the top row to the bottom row. The boxes represent time running out for Kallamehr; they do not correspond to an exact length of time. Two of the time boxes have numbers in them. Wherever you are when you reach these (i.e. when you tick them off), you should make a note of your current paragraph number, then turn at once to the paragraph number given in the box.

You will find it easy to be diverted from the true path throughout this adventure. On your first attempt you will probably run out of time – or even meet with an untimely end. To succeed, you will have to think hard about each choice you make. You will succeed in the adventure only if you do the *right* things at the *right* times. No matter how weak your *Initial* die-rolls, it should be fairly easy to complete the adventure – if you can find the true path!

ADVENTURE SHEET

SKILL	STAMINA	LUCK
Initial	*Initial*	*Initial*
Skill =	*Stamina =*	*Luck =*

ITEMS OF EQUIPMENT CARRIED	GOLD
	JEWELS
	POTIONS
	PROVISIONS REMAINING

MONSTER ENCOUNTER BOXES

Skill = Stamina =	Skill = Stamina =	Skill = Stamina =
Skill = Stamina =	Skill = Stamina =	Skill = Stamina =
Skill = Stamina =	Skill = Stamina =	Skill = Stamina =
Skill = Stamina =	Skill = Stamina =	Skill = Stamina =

BACKGROUND

These are troubled times in Kallamehr. No sooner had its ruler, Lady Carolina, got over the death of her husband than she was flung into a war with the rival trading state Alkemis. After a sea-battle in which many lives were lost, it seemed that Kallamehr had prevailed. Yet there was more to come. Rumours spread of armies massing on the northern borders. Bei-Han, never a friendly neighbour, was said to be preparing for an invasion. Acting decisively, Lady Carolina ordered all her armies to the northern borders. The mountain passes on the borders could be defended with ease. If the armies of Bei-Han were allowed to reach the wide plains of Kallamehr, however, they would wreak untold damage.

You arrive in Kallamehr just as the last troop of soldiers are departing. You find yourself in a city strangely deserted. Life goes on, but without the many brightly costumed warriors who used to parade so proudly down Kallamehr's winding streets. With the soldiers gone, the criminals thrive. You bar the door of your room at night, and sleep with your sword beside your bed.

A few weeks pass. Then, one morning, a wild-eyed messenger rides into the city, yelling incoherent warnings of an invasion from the east. Less than an hour after he disappears into the palace, a servant brings you a note on stationery bearing the seal of the House of Rangor. It is a summons to appear before Lady Carolina herself! It seems your fame as an adventurer has reached her, and in these dark days the Lady has need of fearless warriors.

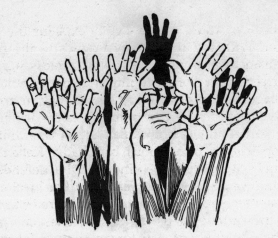

When you arrive at the palace, you find yourself in the company of ten other adventurers. Several are known to you by sight, and one, Sophia of Blacksand, by name, as you have shared dangers with her on more than one occasion. Before you have a chance to exchange names and greetings with the others, you are led inside by a servant. You are ushered into an audience-chamber to face five nobles behind a huge black wooden table. In the centre sits Lady Carolina, resplendent in ceremonial jewellery, the Sword of Office on the table before her. To her left is her cousin Madhaerios, a fat fellow with a nervous twitch in his nose. Beyond him sits Dunyazad of Ikhtiyan, a small woman who is reputed to be the wealthiest person in Kallamehr province. To Carolina's right are Sige the Silent, an imposing woman of ancient lineage, and Asiah Albudur, the stern-faced Judge. Truly you face the five most important people in Kallamehr!

You bow, and Carolina swiftly explains the situation. With the army many leagues to the north, Kallamehr lies unguarded. Now a messenger has arrived from the easternmost regions, telling of villages found deserted. It seems that an army is advancing on the city from the east – it must be barbarian raiders from Kulak Isle. A rider must be dispatched at once to fetch back half of Kallamehr's army. Meanwhile the city must be defended in some way. Carolina explains that her loyal champion Ramedes the Invincible, most feared warrior in all the southern lands, is away on a quest for a fabled relic. She praises you all for your past gallantry and asks that you help her – and gain the gratitude of the whole province – by undertaking the defence of the city. You may be few in number, but surely the glory will be all the greater?

NOW TURN TO PARAGRAPH 1

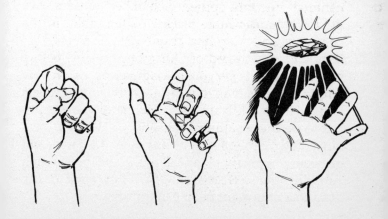

How can you refuse such an appeal? The other ten are quick to volunteer for the task, and your voice joins theirs in pledging allegiance to Lady Carolina. This is your chance to become more than a wandering adventurer – you'll be a true hero of legend! You listen as the five nobles begin to lay plans. One of you must ride to the northern passes and summon the army, another must ride east to scout out the invaders. The rest must remain in Kallamehr and use all their wits and ingenuity to prepare a defence. What do you intend to do:

Volunteer to ride north
for the army?   Turn to **92**

Volunteer to scout to
the east?   Turn to **104**

Remain behind to defend
the city?   Turn to **288**

2

Holding Mema's sticky hand, you make your way back to your horse. You will have to deliver her safely back to her parents, and she tells you that she knows the way to their village. It is back the way you have already come, but to leave her unprotected would not be the action of a hero. Meanwhile she is still covered in the green slime. If you decide to wash it off her, turn to **170**. Otherwise, turn to **396**.

Beneath your feet the crystal surface begins to roughen and slope upwards. More Ectovults pass screeching by, and you scramble up on to the rim of a crater. Looking down, you see a bowl-shaped depression, made of smooth veined rock, with regular grooves. A warm glow radiates from golden sand strewn in its middle. If you wish to go down into the bowl, turn to **103**. If you wish to wait and see if anything happens, turn to **330**.

4

Fourga is the god of pride, and his priests here in
Hasrah certainly have their fair share! The old man
who admits you to the Temple looks you up and
down coldly, saying not a word. You are led in to
see the High Priest, a wrinkled, venerable old fellow
who eyes you with distaste. 'So, the lone dog dares
to darken our portals once more with its presence!'
he snarls in a voice surprisingly firm for one of his
age. 'Perhaps you would care to empty your backpack for us?' If you agree to empty your backpack,
turn to **15**. If you refuse, turn to **390**.

5

You ride northward into the mountains, making
your way carefully through wiry, bleached grass.
There are no paths in these parts, and the grass
conceals pot-holes and ruts. Without guide or mar-
ker you have no way of knowing whether you are
travelling in the right direction, so you trust to your
instincts and keep the sun to your left all the time.
Finally you top a peak and gaze down at a cheerless
plateau. The grass thins out and your heart sinks at
the sight of the barren plain which stretches almost
to the horizon. Then you spot something, far out in
the middle of the plain. Screwing up your eyes, you
stare intently at a small dot – perhaps a hut or other
dwelling. You spur your steed down the slope and,
after a few hours' ride, are at the fringes of the plain.
You realize with alarm that the wind is rising.
Without vegetation, the soil on this plain is dry and
sandy, and it whips up around you, obscuring your

vision and stinging your face. Your horse rears, terrified, and you tumble from the saddle, your right foot tangling in its stirrup. *Test your Luck*. If you are Unlucky, turn to **54**. If you are Lucky, turn to **77**.

6

As you charge him, the Troll pulls the sapling from the hole and uses it as a club.

TROLL   SKILL 9   STAMINA 9

If you defeat him, turn to **207**.

7

You are beginning to feel that you are going to spend the rest of your life in the saddle. The weather is strangely humid for the time of year, and the occasional gusts of wind from the east bring little comfort; they are tainted by a fetid, sickly-sweet stench. The road passes through a jumble of massive boulders and a jagged scarp rises on your left. Ahead of you, another settlement huddles beneath a huge overhang of rock. Strangely, no smoke rises from it. As you approach, you notice several objects littering the road: shoes, bowls and tools. You dismount and enter the village cautiously, finding a desolate street, empty of people and littered with debris. From one of the buildings to your right you can hear a faint knocking sound. Will you:

Follow the knocking?   Turn to **349**

Search the buildings to your left?   Turn to **128**

Hurry out of the village and
    press on?   Turn to 22

8

You open up Sige's pomander and take the herbs
out. You stuff them in your mouth and wince at
the acrid taste, but are rewarded by a spreading
warmth. Make a note that you have eaten the herbs.
If you now examine the items strewn about, turn to
87. If you make your way through the mist, turn
to **116**.

9

You fall immediately into a deep sleep and dream of
a black-clad figure hovering above your bed. Its face
moves down towards you, and it draws back its
hood to reveal the chubby, beaming features of the
innkeeper. Then it reaches up with clawed hands
and peels away its fleshy façade. Beneath the mask,
Sophia of Blacksand leers down at you. Then her
features too are peeled away, revealing the stern
glare of your father! The hands claw again and
again, revealing Madhaerios, Carolina, Dunyazad
and countless other faces drawn from your memory. Finally they pause. Then the last mask is ripped
away. Your own features stare back at you. Tick off a
time box and turn to **28**.

10

As you lie panting, Ramedes grunts and flexes his
broad shoulders. 'I just can't understand it,' he
says, shaking his head. 'Three months ago I was

sent by my Lady on a journey – a mission to retrieve a mighty relic. I braved perils beyond description to find the artefact . . . and my reward? Drugged, beaten and abandoned to that creature by some cowardly pretender. By the Grace of Castis, I had already hidden my prize safely. Now I must deliver it to the Lady Carolina.' With a shock you realize that Ramedes has not learnt of the death of the Lady. You gently explain the truth to him. He clenches his fists and stifles a cry. 'I will have my revenge!' he hisses, 'and I will take it now!' He jumps to his feet and makes his way out of the chamber, grabbing a torch from the wall to light his way along the dark passage. You follow him out of the building and into the courtyard, where he strides over to the water-trough by the stables. He reaches into the scummy water and retrieves a leather pouch. 'I believe I can trust you,' he says, tossing the pouch over to you. 'I go now to root out the traitor who has slain my Lady. Keep this well and, if I should die, give it to Kallamehr's new ruler.' He whirls the flaming brand about his head and charges towards the gate of the keep. If you follow Ramedes, turn to **224**. If you hide in the stables and wait to see what happens, turn to **359**.

11

You tear a strip of cloth from your breeches and tip the leaves on to it. Chopping a small branch from a nearby tree, you wrap the leaf-filled cloth round one end and bind it tight. If you then decide to light the Jheera torch, turn to **34**. If you ride down to meet the army with it unlit, turn to **368**.

12

You forge ahead further into the heart of the forest. The trees seem to close in on you, crowding out the sunlight. The forest floor is now carpeted with rotting leaves, and you find yourself making moderate progress on this springy turf. The atmosphere is close and humid, and you begin to wheeze with the effort. Walking in this weather is exhausting. Lose 1 point of STAMINA as the hours of trudging pass. Finally, you come upon a fork. If you take the right-hand path, turn to **366**. If you take the left-hand path, turn to **273**.

13

The ox lying before you is horribly mutilated; a grey slime seems to have eaten into its flesh. Involuntarily you gag, and turn your eyes away from the foul sight. As you do so, you notice something lying in the grass near by – something pink, resembling an uneven shallow bowl. Curious, you pick it up and discover that it is a mask. When you turn it over you stare at it in disbelief. Your own face, modelled in soft wax, stares back at you! You crumble the

imposter's mask in your hand and fling it angrily
away. Turn to **139**.

14

You feel a sharp pain in your stomach. The thick,
viscous broth was heavy when it slipped down your
throat, but now it is solidifying. You retch, and
begin to shake violently. Then you fall to the
ground. Your adventure ends here.

15

You tip all your possessions out on to the floor
before the High Priest, wondering what the old fool
is trying to prove. Priests of Fourga aren't usually
quite so arrogant. If you have the Golden Fist, turn
to **73**. If you don't have the Fist, turn to **379**.

16

Mema shrieks as the black cloud rises and swims
through the air towards you like a black velvet
shroud. Panic overwhelms you and you wrench
violently at your reins. Mema is nearly swept off the
horse's back as you whirl around and race off. Just
as you think you are safely away, a steady metallic
buzzing reaches your ears. You risk a glance behind
you, and see that the black cloud is gaining on you.
Seconds later it is above you, and then darkness
descends. Turn to **336**.

17

The path begins to slope down, and you hear the
sound of running water from up ahead. Soon you

reach the banks of a fast-flowing stream. After a while, you hear a crashing sound from the far bank. A large and ugly Troll is battering his way through the undergrowth which lines the river bank, towing behind him a green, leafy sapling. If you swim across the river to attack the Troll, turn to **233**. If you have a crossbow, and wish to try to shoot the Troll, turn to **147**. If you remain quietly where you are, turn to **180**.

18

You claw and scrape your way up the wall of the pit with the Quagrant sucking and gurgling behind you. Soon you, like Ramedes, are dangling from the grille. He is tired and probably drugged, however, so you must open the trapdoor yourself. You swing your way over to the trapdoor, but just as you reach it there is a cackle from above. A heavy booted foot stamps on your fingertips. You shriek in pain and drop . . . straight into the gullet of the creature below. Your adventure ends here.

19

Kallamehr is less than a day's ride away, so you put aside your aches for the good of its people and send for your horse. The ostler charges you 1 Gold Piece for stabling (deduct this from your *Adventure Sheet*), but your mare looks well-fed and eager to be off. Before you leave, Barolo hands you a bundle wrapped in an oily rag. 'A little something to match up with your sword,' he says. Unwrapping it, you find it is a small shield – a buckler. It is perfectly balanced for use with your sword, and adds 1 point to your SKILL in combat. If you wish to give Barolo something in return, turn to **134**. Otherwise you wave goodbye to your old teacher and set off. Tick off a time box and turn to **290**.

20

You can hold your breath no longer. The oily black water floods into your lungs, and the tentacles claim their victim.

21

Pressing straight on, you find the undergrowth creeping on to the path ahead of you. Soon it becomes difficult to push your way through it. You laboriously hack your way through (lose 1 point of STAMINA), finally reaching a clearing from which two other paths lead. If you take the path on the left, turn to **366**. If you take the path on the right, turn to **221**.

22

Leaving the village and its mighty rock outcrop behind, you follow the road. A few miles further on, you come upon another village, as deserted as the last. Search though you may, you can find no explanation for the sudden disappearance of its inhabitants. There are signs of fighting – broken furniture, footprints milling about in the dust of the main street – but no signs of bloodshed, and no corpses. Your mission was to discover the nature and the weaknesses of the enemy, yet so far it has just meant more and more mystery. Tick off a time box. If you carry on riding eastwards, turn to **91**. If you turn round and go back the way you came, turn to **223**.

23

Pocketing the scrap, you listen attentively as Dunyazad suggests that you stick to the roads. Though they will carry you a roundabout way, they will be far quicker than chancing a ride across country. When you have left the table and are alone, you examine the scrap of paper. It reads: 'Beware – you are watched by a thousand eyes.' Turn to **140**.

24

It is not easy swimming against the current, but you finally struggle back to the bank and drag yourself out of the water like a drowned rat. You shake some of the water off you, then brave the tunnel. Turn to **362**.

25

You are just about to unhook the rope from the spike it was wrapped round when you notice a guardsman coming along the walkway. He hasn't spotted you yet, but he will be passing very close to you. If you flatten yourself against the roof, in the hope that he won't spot you, turn to **272**. If you have a crossbow and wish to shoot the guard, turn to **39**. If you slide down the rope to the shadows of the courtyard below, turn to **99**.

You have been riding for several hours when you are forced to rein in by a battered fellow who staggers on to the road ahead of you and collapses in a heap. You dismount to see what the trouble is. Between gasps, he tells you his misfortune: 'I, the legendary Tasbadh, doer of mighty deeds, slayer of Evil, and seeker of truths, find myself staring Death full in the face. I should never have incurred the wrath of the Dark Jester by seeking to foil his evil plottings. 'Tis true, I levelled his palace and banished his warped minions from this plane. Yet a fool I was to believe this would truly vanquish one so steeped in Evil. Even as I was making my way from the ruins, his tentacles of malice were reaching out to envelop me. Through the greatest love of my life, whom I trusted implicitly, he wrought his foul revenge. A Death Spell is pulsing through my sinews, and even *my* iron constitution cannot resist it much longer. My only hope is the Healer of Gebaan, but I cannot go on without food – and even then the Healer has his price and I have no money. That I, Keeper of the Fabled Fortune of Foraznak, should die for want of four Gold Pieces!' His head sinks wearily upon his shoulders, and he sobs. Tick off a time box. Will you:

Give him the money and Provisions he craves?	Turn to **177**
Leave him to his fate and ride on?	Turn to **308**
Question him further?	Turn to **88**

27

The chariot seems to be the only way out of this wasteland, but how do you get on to it? If you wrap yourself in the Gatherer's robe, take his silken bag and approach it, turn to **212**. If you wish to overpower the Crystal Sprite, turn to **179**.

28

You awake with a start. You are gagging violently on a mouthful of acrid smoke. The whole room is full of it, lit by a red glow from beyond the door. Holding the bedsheet over your face, you stumble from the bed over to the shuttered windows. You fling them open and recoil in horror. Outside the window hovers a black-clad figure. Beneath its dark hood, the fiery red glow from the door is reflected back at you, split into a hundred glinting jewels. Your ears are assailed by a loud buzzing and you lash out at the figure with your fist. It is too quick for you, and shoots vertically upwards. Will you:

Run for the door?	Turn to **61**
Climb out of the window?	Turn to **304**
Look for another way out?	Turn to **167**

29

As you sit and wait, drowsiness overcomes you. When you wake, the sun has crossed the sky. Tick off a time box. If anyone has entered or left the hut, you have missed them. You decide to waste no more time. If you walk under the hut, turn to **254**. If you climb up one of the legs, turn to **202**.

30

When you suggest that the guards might let you into the palace, you are met by blank stares. They tell you once more to come back the next day, and deny all knowledge of the money you have given them. If you give them some more Gold Pieces, note down the number, then turn to **327**. If you threaten them, turn to **210**. If you abandon your attempt to enter the palace, turn to **130**.

31

Check the names of the herbs in the pomander, as marked on your *Adventure Sheet*. Replace each letter with the corresponding number from the key below. Then add up the numbers that go to make each name. Taking the words in the order you have them written down will give you a three-figure number. Turn to the paragraph corresponding to this number.

P = 0	A = 1	T = 2	E = 1
U = 2	H = 0	M = 3	Q = 4

Alternatively, you may flee by turning to **335**.

32

The trail ploughs straight through the trees, and you traipse along it for an hour before the monotony is relieved by a branching of the ways. If you go right, turn to **123**. If you go left, turn to **312**.

33

You struggle to clear your mind of the fearful visions which beset it. You feel as if molten metal is running through your veins. You get no rest this night. Lose 2 points of STAMINA and 1 point of SKILL. Next morning you bid Barolo an abrupt farewell, retrieve your horse from the stables (pay the ostler 1 Gold Piece), and depart, slumped in the saddle. Tick off a time box and turn to **290**.

34

You strike a spark from your tinder-box on to the torch, so that the cloth begins to smoulder. Soon the acrid fumes of the Jheera are wafting from it. With your weapon prepared, you ride forth. Turn to **368**.

35

Mema clings on for dear life as you spur your horse towards the village. As you approach the palisade, the large gates swing open, and you are beckoned in by a worried villager. Mema slips down from the horse and rushes into the arms of her parents. You waste no time in telling the people of the danger they are in. They grab what they can of their possessions and livestock before fleeing. Finally, you find yourself alone outside the deserted village. The huge black army is in sight now, steadily oozing down the valley towards you. It is time to make your own escape. Turn to **53**.

36

You land in a bowl-shaped crater in the ground. As you lie there, stunned, six Crystal Warriors carrying huge crystal hammers climb over the rim of the crater and advance towards you. If you have your sword, turn to **201**. Otherwise, turn to **168**.

37

You step back in revulsion at the sight of a slimy green form crouched within the cupboard. It holds a slender tube to its mouth, which it points at your face. Looking closer, you see frightened eyes fixed on you. This is no creature of evil, but a young girl, coated from head to foot in a sticky, foul-smelling mire. You smile at her encouragingly, and she lowers her makeshift blow-pipe as she realizes you mean her no harm. Gently, you hold out your hand and take the blow-pipe from her, pocketing it to keep it out of harm's way. 'Who are you?' you ask her. Turn to **315**.

38

You burst from the trees and find yourself teetering on the brink of a gorge. Staring with horror down into its depths, you feel the earth crumbling beneath your feet. As you feel yourself toppling towards your death, you flail desperately about you. Your hands make contact with a straggly tree-root and you grasp it for dear life. You are dashed painfully against the wall of the chasm (lose 2 points of STAMINA), but manage to keep your grip. With some effort, you pull yourself back up to safety and rest. There is no sign of your quarry – he has vanished into thin air. Turn to **139**.

39

Quickly you wind the string back and load a bolt. You wait until the guard is silhouetted against the moon before shooting. Roll two dice. If the result is *less than* your SKILL, turn to **118**. If the result is *greater than or equal to* your SKILL, turn to **84**.

40

You make your way stealthily round the edge of the crater. A short distance away to one side, you can see a crystal chariot with two Ectovults tethered to it and a Crystal Sprite standing patiently by. You hide behind a crystal outcrop until the cowled Gatherer approaches. If you leap out and strike at him with your sword, turn to **85**. If you challenge him, turn to **154**.

41

Gripping your sword in both hands, you twirl it about you like a scythe. Two priests fall, and the others shrink back. You make for the door, but the priests raise their staves and close in. You flail desperately, but there are too many of them. Their blows rain down upon your head. Your adventure ends here.

42

With the cloud close behind you, you spur your horse down the valley and into the river with a splash. Unfortunately, the frothing water unseats you, and the Jheera torch is doused. As you struggle to keep yourself afloat, the hornets descend on you. You dive beneath the water to avoid them, but your breath cannot last for ever. When you break the surface, gasping, they are there, stings poised to strike . . . Turn to **336**.

43

You vault on to the platform and confront the four nobles. You begin by demanding justice, and tell them how they have been misled by a traitor – but a shout cuts you off. "Ware, assassin! shouts Luthaur, drawing his sword and leaping for you. The nobles cower back in their ornate seats. You must defend yourself against Luthaur's furious attack.

LUTHAUR   SKILL 8   STAMINA 17

As soon as you take a wound in the fight, turn to **143**. If you defeat Luthaur without taking a wound, turn to **169**.

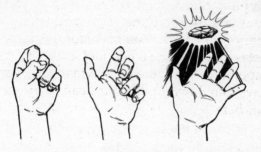

44

Tired though you are, you cannot sleep. You remember Sige's promise that the pomander would prevent you sleeping, but surely this has become more a hindrance than a help? Your body cries out for true rest, squirming in tortured agony at lack of sleep. If you decide to remove the pomander in the hope that this will help you sleep, turn to **382**. If not, turn to **278**.

45

The broth tastes foul as it slides sluggishly down your throat, then settles unpleasantly in your stomach. You brace yourself against the goblet and take a few deep breaths. If you have drunk the potion labelled 'Arahl', or added it to the broth, turn to **14**. If you added the potion marked 'Zazzaz' to the broth, turn to **90**. Otherwise, turn to **68**.

46

The sword swishes past your back as you roll to the right, grabbing your sword as you go. You leap to your feet and parry the next blow. Your opponent is a Black Elf, and behind him you see two more of his kind.

First BLACK ELF   SKILL 7   STAMINA 6

If you win, turn to **120**.

47

Dunyazad sits up in her seat and stares at you. Then she makes her way stiffly over to the coffin. She pauses for a moment. 'I know what you are trying to prove,' she says icily, 'but what would *I* have to gain from murdering one who has protected my interests well?' She bends forward and gently kisses Carolina's pale lips. There is silence in the courtyard. All eyes are on Carolina. But there is no change in the colour of her lips. Dunyazad turns to the guards and says quietly, 'Arrest the presumptuous dog.' Before you can defend yourself they are upon you. Turn to **355**.

48

You join the Murkurons at the door and brace yourself against it. Then the fourth Murkuron squawks, 'Isbech Pinzha!' His comrades dive away from the door, with you close behind. The door bursts open and squat reptilian shapes pile into the room. There is a flash, an intense burst of heat, and when you open your eyes the floor is littered with charred Kokomokoa. The Murkurons spring to their feet and dash through the door, the magician bowing to you politely before joining the others. They charge down the tunnel ahead of you, only to return seconds later, shrieking. You dodge them as they pass and, nervously, follow the tunnel until it opens into a large chamber. Turn to **82**.

49

When you tell them that you were sent out by Lady Carolina personally, they raise their eyebrows and look you up and down. One of them disappears inside the palace while the other still bars your way.

After some while the first one reappears. 'They're too busy with the Lady Carolina's funeral arrangements to see you today – you'll have to come back tomorrow. I suggest you have a bath, too, if you want to be allowed in.' If you wish to bribe the guards, note down how much you propose giving them, then turn to **387**. If you wish to threaten them with your sword, turn to **210**. Otherwise you must take their advice and go back to the town. Turn to **130**.

The woman cackles, and the vision disappears. 'No, I am not he, though I know him. He was my last visitor, and his vision was the same as yours. My name is Aletheia.' As she speaks, you feel a soft weight drop upon your shoulder. You turn your head to find yourself staring into the eyes of a serpent. You shudder and automatically grab for it. But it is too fast for you. In an instant its thick coils are wrapped around your neck. 'Meet Caduceus,' says the woman. Turn to **307**.

51

You unsling your crossbow and load a bolt. You cannot make out the beast clearly in the pit below. You let fly the bolt into the darkness, and are rewarded by the sound of a throaty squawk; it has been injured, but it is still alive. The dangling man moans hoarsely and his grip loosens. If you take another shot at the beast, turn to **303**. If you abandon the crossbow and try to open the trapdoor, turn to **162**.

52

Most of the occupants of the frozen cocoon are long since dead, their mummified faces contorted with agony. But as you approach the source of the whispering, your left hand tingles. Within one of the crystal statues you make out the features of Sige, and you can now hear her whisper: 'Free me! I can help you defeat Bythos. He has cheated me of my destiny and left me here to rot with his other failed agents.' If you wish to smash the crystal and free Sige, turn to **286**. If you would prefer to leave her, turn to **75**.

53

The black horde is behind you. It is still many miles from Kallamehr, yet it is engulfing everything in its path. Although you know of no weakness in the enemy, surely Kallamehr should be forewarned: evacuation may be the only means of survival. Tick off a time box. Will you:

Ride to warn Kallamehr?	Turn to **129**
Try to find out more about the enemy?	Turn to **325**
Search for Enthymesis the Enchanter (if you recognize the name)?	Turn to **5**

54

Your horse bolts, dragging you helplessly some distance before you are finally battered unconscious. Lose 2 points of STAMINA and tick off a time box. When you come round, the sandstorm is subsiding. Turn to **98**.

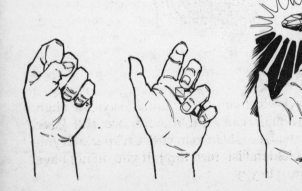

55

As you take the fish-shaped bottle out of your pack, your opponent shrinks back. He stretches his hand out towards you and moans, 'No! No! Not that!' You ignore his pleas and uncork the bottle. There is a sound like a faint chuckle from within, and the once-proud commander of the army dissolves into helpless crazed laughter. If you know the Spitting Fly and wish to use it, turn to **255**. If you wish to draw your sword and attack him, turn to **324**.

56

'You are wise to change your mind,' says the High Priest. 'Though we are old now, we still have power. Let us see what lies in your backpack.' If you have the Golden Fist, turn to **73**. If you do not have the Fist, turn to **379**.

57

Suddenly you are taken by surprise by a black hooded shape, which leaps on your back, digging its bony hands into your shoulders. As you twist to hurl the shape off, something lances into your leg and agony shoots through you. Lose 3 points of STAMINA. You hurl the shape from you and prepare to do battle. Your opponent flings back his hood and you find yourself face to face with a huge hornet, its faceted eyes glittering back at you. It jerks and twitches sickeningly as you close in.

HORNET ASSASSIN   SKILL 5   STAMINA 10

If you do not have your sword you fight at −2 and may not score *killing blows*. If you defeat the Hornet, turn back to the paragraph you came from.

58

Two paths lead out of the glade, one to your left and one to your right. You are just deciding which way to go when you are startled by an ant-eater which waddles out of a clump of orchids and foxgloves to your left, making straight for the mound in the middle of the glade. Wishing him a hearty meal, you continue on your way. If you have three numbers written on your *Adventure Sheet*, turn to the paragraph they indicate. Otherwise, if you go along the right-hand path, write the number '1' after any other numbers on your *Adventure Sheet* and turn to **17**. If you go along the left-hand path, write the number '2' after any other numbers on your *Adventure Sheet* and turn to **388**. If you already have one of these numbers written down, you should choose the other option.

59

You dislodge the cask and grasp the iron ring of the trapdoor. No sooner have you jerked the trapdoor open than a pair of arms shoot out, your legs are tugged sharply and you tumble down a short flight of stone steps, landing with a splash. You black out. You are brought round by a stinging blow to your head. Deduct 1 STAMINA point. Your mouth is full of warm vinegared wine. You are sitting in a lake of the stuff a foot deep and facing you is a bedraggled wretch who swings at you once more with surprising vigour. Choking on the wine, you dodge his blow and stagger to your feet. You must defend yourself!

WRETCH   SKILL 6   STAMINA 8

If you defeat him, turn to **222**.

60

You have solved the Troll's indigestion problem quite effectively – he lies dead at your feet. Giving him no further thought, you make your way back to the trail which runs along the river bank. Turn to **133**.

61

You hastily snatch up your possessions and wrap your hand in the bedsheet. You curse when you find the door is locked. You kick hard at the middle panel of the door, and are rewarded as it collapses in a pile of charred matchwood. Then a greedy tongue of flame licks through the opening and engulfs you. Your clothes catch alight instantly. Your adventure ends here.

62

Your weapon enables you to damage the warrior, but it is a formidable opponent. You may not strike *killing blows* against it.

CRYSTAL WARRIOR   SKILL 11   STAMINA 13

You may *Escape* after one round (turn to **346**). If you defeat the Crystal Warrior, turn to **398**.

63

You tether your horse and see to her feed. Lighting a small fire for protection, you settle yourself down for the night. Hours pass as you gaze up at the constellations above you. You remember Sige explaining her pomander's power to arrest sleep. You are grateful for its properties when you observe several stealthy forms approaching. You lie still, feigning sleep, your hand inches from your sword-hilt. If you wait until they are nearly upon you before attacking, turn to **214**. If you leap up before they advance further, turn to **348**.

64

On the grille above you stands the spindly jailer, cackling and dangling the keys from his fingers. You must find a way of killing him quickly if you are to get out of this accursed pit. If you know the Spitting Fly and wish to use it, turn to **259**. If you have a crossbow and wish to use it, turn to **186**. If you have a blow-pipe which has not been used before and wish to use it, turn to **197**. Otherwise, turn to **352**.

65

You charge him, yelling your battle-cry. He blocks your first slash effortlessly, and then launches one of his own. You only half parry it, flinching under the impact. You are completely outclassed – he counters every blow instantly, while the steely eyes which are locked on yours betray no sign of his own moves. Finally you sink to your knees, unable to resist the onslaught. 'I will be Master of this land as I am Master of the Abyss,' he says, 'and none are left to stop me.' His sword scythes down.

66

Outside in the twilight you see the villagers gathered around someone who is talking in a scratchy, high-pitched voice. This must be a wise woman or perhaps a witch, for the villagers are listening respectfully to her witterings. Then she whirls and points a scabby finger at you. 'It is that one!' she screeches. 'The prophecy of the winged messenger is fulfilled! Our Protector has come to save us from the creeping horde! Tell us that you will stay with us and deliver us from evil.' If you agree to the old woman's demands, turn to 208. If you tell her she is mistaken, turn to 160.

67

You spur your horse once more to a gallop, race through the city gates and along the Way of Flint to the palace. There you confront two of the palace guard, the only soldiers left in the city. 'State your business, peasant,' one of them grunts, 'we have no need of kitchen hands.' You step back in astonishment at their impudence. Surely they must know of you? If you insist that you are on a vital mission, turn to 49. If you decide to draw your sword and threaten the guardsmen, turn to 210.

68

The door at the far end of the chamber slams open deafeningly, and in strides Bythos. This is not the Bythos you killed earlier, but a towering giant, fully fifty feet tall. His gaunt, leering features are all the more threatening for their size, and his elegant robes billow about his huge frame. If you smashed the goblet, turn to **149**. Otherwise, turn to **225**.

69

Mema shrieks as the black cloud rises and moves towards you, swimming through the air like a black velvet shroud. You are overcome by panic and you wrench violently at your steed's reins. Mema is nearly swept off the horse's back as you whirl around and race off. You risk a glance behind you, and see the black cloud swarming after you. A metallic buzzing fills your ears. As it approaches, you realize that it is a swarm of black hornets, each the size of a locust. As they swirl above your head, you brace yourself for the impact, but it never comes. You gallop on, hoping against hope that you will have time to get all the villagers clear before the hornets arrive. Turn to **35**.

70

Taking care to keep out of sight, you trail the army as it sweeps across the countryside. Before it enters the next village, the black cloud rises from the palanquin and descends upon the settlement. Soon after, the villagers emerge and join the growing horde. The same fate befalls other villages in the army's path, until eventually Kallamehr itself is in sight. You have failed the city – your cowardice has condemned it to destruction.

71

You creep along the walkway until you reach the point where it meets the keep. From here it is only a short drop on to the slightly sloping roof of the keep of the palace. Above you rises the keep's tower; but you devote your attention to the keep below. The winged creature came from one of the windows below, but you're not certain which one. The keep has four walls looking into the courtyard, and each has a small casement window. Around the edge of the keep runs a row of ornamental spikes, round which you will be able to loop the rope. You will be able to lower yourself down the wall to peer in at each of the windows. Which wall do you lower yourself down first:

The far left wall?	Turn to 397
The left centre wall?	Turn to 94
The right centre wall?	Turn to 218
The far right wall?	Turn to 340

72

Suddenly you hear a croak from near by. You turn towards the noise and see a human face, embedded in a greenish slime. 'You must flee,' it says feebly. 'I, Enthymesis, have failed to slay Maijem-Nosoth. I have little time left to live, but you must escape. Do not go near the sands; they lead to the Abyss!

Hurry, the beast returns!' If you hurry back down the passage which brought you here, turn to **230**. If you make for the centre of the chamber, turn to **263**.

73

As the golden statuette tumbles out of your backpack, a sigh goes up from the priests. 'Caught red-handed!' snaps the High Priest. A priest lifts the Golden Fist reverently from the ground and places it carefully on a plinth in the centre of the Temple. His fellows then join him in a circle around it, and they begin to chant. As the priests seem to have temporarily forgotten you, you would like to make a stealthy exit from the Temple, but your feet are rooted to the spot. The priests' chanting swells, and a warm green glow begins to seep through the fingers of the Fist. As you watch, the fingers uncurl, revealing a green gem. It floats lazily above the now open palm of the golden hand. Its glow is too bright for you to bear. Then it subsides, and you find yourself free to move. The priests have been transformed; no longer heavy with years, now they are young, fit fighting-priests. Two of them break from the circle and gesture for you to accompany them. They lead you down a corridor to a cell. Cross the Golden Fist off your possessions. Turn to **353**.

74

Madhaerios flushes bright crimson, then bursts into tears. Rising from his seat, he totters over to the coffin and plants his puffy lips on those of his dead cousin. Then, quivering all over, he returns to his seat and collapses into it. Carolina's lips retain their pallor, and the crowd begins to mutter. 'How dare you be so tactless,' says Dunyazad. She turns to the guards and says quietly, 'Arrest the presumptuous dog.' Before you can defend yourself they are upon you. Turn to 355.

75

Leaving the crystal statues to their frozen contemplation, you press on into the mist. Soon you can hear an ominous creaking from up ahead. Turn to 237.

76

You just have enough time to glimpse a small, slimy green form, cramped within the cupboard, before you are engulfed in a choking cloud of gritty powder. You drop your sword and clutch at your face. Your eyes burn, your nose starts to run and you retch violently (lose 1 point of STAMINA). Then whatever was in the cupboard comes tumbling out and worms its way between your legs. If you wish to make a grab at it, roll two dice. If the result is *less than* your SKILL, turn to 172. If the result is *greater than or equal to* your SKILL, or if you don't want to grab the creature, turn to 194.

77

Though you land painfully, you manage to grasp the stirrup in your hands, and tug at it to calm your panicking mare. Grabbing her reins and bridle, you force her to the ground and hide behind her while the sandstorm rages around you. You wait for the wind to subside. Turn to **98**.

78

Your sword flashes from its scabbard and you advance on the vast figure. 'Impertinent fool!' he bellows, and lets loose a freezing blast. Crystals form on your skin, but quickly melt away, leaving Bythos momentarily at a loss. However, he soon rallies and rapidly fashions a sword from crystal. Against such a huge and skilful opponent you cannot possibly prevail, and you die heroically here, battling to the very end.

79

The Winged Assassin lets out a choked hiss and reels backwards and up. You have no time to follow its erratic flight, as the heat in the room is now overpowering. Will you:

Run for the door?	Turn to **61**
Climb out of the window?	Turn to **262**
Look for another way out?	Turn to **323**

80

The vision disappears. The woman claps her hands and smiles. 'You are bright, for all your ragged looks. It seems destiny has guided you this far, so I must play my part in its design. Many trials lie before you, and your enemy is not easily vanquished. But Bythos has fears, and you may be his nemesis. Enthymesis has gone on ahead of you, and his aid will be invaluable.' If you have Sige's pomander, turn to **295**. If you do not, turn to **114**.

81

As your mount crashes to the ground, you leap from her back. Although you land heavily, you are unharmed. Sadly, the same cannot be said for the mare. One of her front legs is twisted. She limps towards you and nuzzles your face, as if to apologize. She cannot be ridden, so you'll have to lead her to the nearest village and get another horse. Turn to **155**.

82

The cavern has a high ceiling, and a fine mist of sand falls from it. The middle of the floor is covered with sand, and quivers slightly. Strewn carelessly across the sand are an assortment of incredible relics and treasures – a magical hoard the like of which you have never seen. With each tremor of the sand they sink deeper. A faint whistling, as of wind in a ravine, reaches your ears. Check the time boxes on your *Adventure Sheet* and turn to the paragraph given below for the number of boxes you have crossed off:

Fewer than 13 boxes	Turn to **72**
13–17 boxes	Turn to **309**
More than 17 boxes	Turn to **343**

83

As you parry the first guard's blow, you almost fall over. Your reactions are dulled from lack of sleep. Reduce your SKILL by 2 points.

	SKILL	STAMINA
First GUARD	7	8
Second GUARD	6	7

You must fight both the guards together. At the beginning of each Attack Round, you must decide which of the two you are going to fight; resolve the battle against him as normal. You should also roll two dice to determine your Attack Strength against the other guard, then two dice again for his Attack Strength against you for that Attack Round. You will not injure him if your Attack Strength is greater: you will simply parry his blow. If his Attack Strength is greater than yours, then he will damage you in the normal way. If you defeat both the guardsmen, turn to 102.

84

Your shot goes wide, striking the wall with a spark some distance behind the guard. He turns, readies his crossbow and edges back along the walkway. You realize that this is your chance to slip away unseen. Turn to 151.

85

You take the Gatherer by surprise, your sword smashing him to the ground. Beneath the cowl is an emaciated, almost skeletal form. Turn to 27.

86

You prepare to battle this terrifying foe. Then you notice a pair of fancy boots poking down through the smoke-hole. They are followed by a gaudily dressed figure who spirals effortlessly down a coiling rope. His billowing, brightly coloured clothing is completely out of place in this grubby hut. The figure bows to you expansively, and hails you. 'Greetings, traveller! I am called the Riddling Reaver, and, as luck would have it, I'm here to rescue you. I've been keeping an eye on you, and since you've made a complete pig's ear of things so far, I've decided to save your bacon. If you waste your time on every peasant who begs you to wipe his nose, then Kallamehr has no chance.' He twitches and giggles to himself. Pointing to the snake-like rope, he says, 'This is the end of the line. So hurry up and get hold of it!' He spirals effortlessly up the rope, just as you hear the bar scrape back from the door behind you. If you grab the rope, turn to **96**. If not, turn to **236**.

87

You cannot begin to count the number of magical items strewn about you. Several catch your eye: a gem-encrusted breastplate (far too small for you), a huge pair of shiny boots (apparently made of feathers), a golden fist, a pearl-inlaid skull, an onyx sceptre and a crystal globe mounted on a velvet plinth. If you wish to take any of these, note down which ones you take on your *Adventure Sheet*. Then you head into the mist. Turn to **116**.

88

Tasbadh continues at length with tales of his own heroic exploits, which grow ever more outrageous. You soon realize that he is beginning to contradict himself, and you wonder if the man is truly suffering from a deadly curse. Tick off a time box. If you agree to give him food and money, turn to **177**. If you doubt his tale and ride off without him, turn to **308**.

89

The river leads into a tunnel in the side of a mountain, and you are swept into darkness. After a short while, the river sweeps round a bend and you are washed up on a rocky shelf, which is worn smooth by the pounding water. As you lie there, sodden and panting, you take a look at your surroundings. A guttering torch has been driven into a crevice near by, and by its light you see that, once round the bend, the river runs beneath an arch. Iron bars are set into the arch, blocking entry. Behind you, leading from the rocky shelf, is a dark tunnel, with light flickering along its walls. If you re-enter the water and examine the bars, turn to **277**. If you investigate the tunnel, turn to **362**.

90

As thunderous steps approach the chamber from the other door, you begin to feel strangely sleepy. Your eyes blur and their lids feel heavy. You slump against the goblet and start to snore. You never wake up.

91

You pass through a string of deserted villages. You are overwhelmed by a sense of isolation, of terrible loneliness, as you travel through this wasteland. How can you save a country all of whose people have vanished with hardly a trace? You lose all sense of time, as there is nothing to mark one day from the next. Your purpose gone, you wander aimlessly. Finally casting your sword away, you meander through the countryside. Your adventure ends here.

92

Before you leave, Lady Carolina gives you a sealed scroll to deliver to Yunan, commander of her army. She wishes you the Luck of Castis on your mission, and directs you to choose the best steed from her

stables. Soon you are galloping away from Kallamehr. Tick off a time box. You have travelled
several leagues and are just thinking of stopping for
a swig of ale from your bottle when your horse
suddenly stumbles. *Test your Luck*. If you are Lucky,
turn to **81**. If you are Unlucky, turn to **192**.

93

The chunk of crystal you are standing on starts to
turn over, and you slide from it into the murky black
liquid. As you flounder towards the crystal floor,
the black shape falls from the clouds and on to the
surface. You have no time to take in its features, for
your leg is grabbed by stinging tentacles and you
slip beneath the water. You will have to fight your
way free. If you do not have your sword, turn to **184**.

TENTACLES	SKILL 6	STAMINA 5

If you are still fighting after four Attack Rounds,
turn to **20**. If you defeat the Tentacles within four
Attack Rounds, turn to **146**.

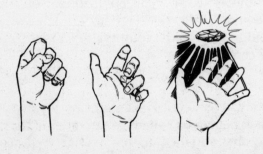

94

You lower yourself slowly down the wall until you are level with the window. Then you crane your head round to peer in. The room is quite sparingly furnished, containing nothing more than a bed, a couple of chairs and a dressing-table with mirror. On the bed, Asiah Albudur sits bolt upright, fully dressed. She stares at one of the empty chairs and seems to be conducting a conversation. You catch brief snatches: '. . . I remember when you first came to Kallamehr and I introduced you to Baron Bluestone. Who would have known then that you were to marry him? . . . Such a sweet innocent young thing, you were . . . What's that? . . . You must stop worrying about Kallamehr, Carolina, I'm sure Madhaerios has everything under control . . .' There's no more you can learn here. You pull yourself back up the wall of the keep. If this is the third window you have looked in, turn to **25**. Otherwise, you may return to your quarters (turn to **151**), or investigate any of the following, if you have not done so already:

The far left wall Turn to **397**
The right centre wall Turn to **218**
The far right wall Turn to **340**

95

Your attention is drawn to the far end of the valley, way off to your right. You shiver involuntarily, and the hairs on the nape of your neck rise. Your horse shies and whinnies in terror. A thick stench fills your lungs. The sparse slopes are being slowly enveloped by an advancing wave of black lava . . . or so it seems. Your eyes adjust to the distance and you see that the oozing black mass is not liquid, but a seething ocean of people. Even as you watch, it seeps closer, spreading like a dark stain. You have found the invading army, but will you survive to make use of your knowledge? There are many more people in the horde below than in Kallamehr's entire army. If you ride down into the valley to take a closer look, turn to **153**. If you gallop off to your left to try to reach the village, turn to **358**.

96

No sooner have you grasped the end of the rope than you are jerked violently off your feet. You are swept upwards and out through the smoke-hole. Below you, the torches of the angry villagers

97

dwindle, and their wails can just be heard through the din. The angry buzzing comes from above, but all you can see is a huge black shadow. You are carried through the air for some way, before being set down with a bump on solid ground. The Reaver spins down the rope and alights near you, and this time he is cradling a peculiarly shaped bottle in his arms. He holds it out to you, and you see that it is shaped like a particularly ugly fish. 'You'll be needing this,' says the Reaver, passing you the bottle. 'In it is a sense of humour which I stole several years ago, in my impetuous youth. You'll be meeting its former owner soon, so you'd better give it back to him: there's nothing so soft as a villain with a sense of humour!' He winks knowingly at you and, without another word, shoots up the rope. The buzzing rises in pitch, and the black shadow drifts off. You are alone, lost, without your horse. Wearily, you settle down to wait out the rest of the night. Turn to **331**.

97

You land deftly, rolling forward to absorb the shock. As you straighten up, you feel your back spattered with some viscous liquid, which begins to bubble and hiss. You tear off your jerkin and fling it into a nearby water-trough. As it hits the water, a plume of steam rises into the air, and the water bubbles furiously. Stepping backwards, you look up cautiously. With an intense whine a black-winged creature rolls high into the air and disappears into the night. Turn to **111**.

98

When the dust finally settles, you find yourself staring at an expanse of forest. Its presence is inexplicable – you saw no sign of it before the sandstorm. Intrigued, you approach and lead your horse along a faintly marked path between the trees, into the silent forest. Soon the narrow path forks at a massive, creeper-strewn tree with drooping foxgloves covering its roots. Looking around, you see the undergrowth is thick and impenetrable, and you resolve to tether your horse here before investigating further. If you take the left-hand path, write down the number '3' on your *Adventure Sheet* and turn to **268**. If you take the right-hand path, write down the number '2' on your *Adventure Sheet* and turn to **388**. If you examine the tree and the plants which cover it, turn to **356**.

99

Slipping back over the spikes, you slide down the rough rope. You land lightly in the courtyard and hurry into the shadows near by, keeping your eye on the guard above you. You look across to the door of the servants' quarters, wondering if you'll be able to make it over there unobserved. Turn to **204**.

100

The bushes give way to nothingness. For a moment you hang on the edge of a precipice, before the earth beneath your feet crumbles away. Then you are hurtling down, down, down. The chasm is very deep. The ground rushes up to meet you . . .

101

'Who?' the woman screeches, the vision disintegrating before you. 'I have no time for tricksters, but you may be more to the taste of my companion.' You feel a soft weight upon your shoulders, and turn to find yourself staring into the eyes of a huge serpent. 'Caduceus! A new plaything for you!' the woman cackles. The snake slithers round your neck before you can grab it and fling it from you. Then, very slowly, the coils tighten. Your adventure ends here.

102

You realize that wearing Sige's pomander has sapped your strength. You remember her words when she gave it to you: 'It is a valuable magical item blessed with the luck of the gods.' 'Which gods?' you wonder, for surely it has brought you more bad fortune than good. If you remove the pomander from around your neck, turn to **355**. If you keep the pomander on, turn to **150**.

103

You edge down the side of the bowl, treading carefully to keep your footing on the slippery rock. As you reach the bottom, six Crystal Warriors carrying huge crystal hammers climb over the rim of the crater and advance on you. Turn to **201**.

104

You are sitting at a table with the five nobles, eating a fine meal to fortify you as they give you your final briefing. They are being waited on by their own servants, while Carolina has assigned one of her pages to take care of you. Madhaerios warns you against taking any incautious action yourself. 'It is most important that you return to tell us of the nature of this menace so that we may know how best to defend against it,' he explains. While Dunyazad is in the middle of advising you to rest at the Temple of Fourga, you feel a light touch on your leg. You look around and see the page who was waiting upon you walking away. Looking down into your lap you see a folded fragment of paper. The page must have dropped this as he refilled your goblet. If you pick it up to read it straight away, turn to **264**. If you slip it into your pocket to read later, turn to **23**.

105

Your sword flashes up to parry. Roll two dice. If the result is *less than* your SKILL, turn to **241**. If it is *greater than or equal to* your SKILL, turn to **274**.

106

Luckily the cave mouth is large enough to take both you and your horse, but a rude shock awaits you within. A pathetic Caveman, clutching a large bone, leaps up to strike you as you enter, knocking the Jheera torch from your hand. You draw your sword and attack.

CAVEMAN   SKILL 7   STAMINA 7

If you defeat him within five Attack Rounds, turn to **144**. If you are still fighting at the end of five Attack Rounds, turn to **181**.

107

Your lungs ache for want of air, and your heart pounds madly as you try to break the hold the creature has on you. But it is to no avail; your arms grow steadily weaker. You gulp in your last mouthful of wine.

108

Bythos topples to the ground, shattering into a myriad tiny fragments. You reel in the chain until the wall of cells breaks through the clouds; you then rip the bars off, freeing its miniature occupants. Thousands upon thousands of them totter feebly out of the cells and mill around, gazing about them in wonderment. When they have all emerged, you lead them back across the crystal wastes to the palace. There you are greeted by the cowled Servants; they bow low and proclaim you the new Ruler of the Abyss. Now you must find a way of returning to Kallamehr, so you ask them how it is done. They tell you that Bythos used a rare blue crystal, powdered and dissolved in water, to travel to the earthly plane. Some remains, stored in the palace, and the Servants set about preparing the potion. Time passes as they complete their task. Finally they present to you a huge vessel full of clear blue liquid. The newly appointed Gatherer steps forward and speaks. 'Majesty, a great quantity of this potion is required to transfer your mighty being. We have prepared as much as we could, but unfortunately there is not enough both for you and for all these spirits to be returned. You must make a choice.' If you drink the blue liquid yourself, turn to **205**. If you divide it among the citizens of Kallamehr, turn to **250**.

109

You follow Tasbadh into the tavern. As you enter, the mighty hero is being threatened by the tavern-keeper who grips him by his jerkin and shouts at him: 'No more drinks for you, you old faker! This'll just about pay off your slate! If you want more booze, then I'll see your money first!' You curse yourself for being fooled by the drunkard, and step back into the street, seething. There's nothing to be done but mount your horse and continue on your journey. Turn to **7**.

110

You draw the locket from its leather pouch and hold it up above your head for all to see. The citizens near you back away in awe. You are about to tell how Ramedes was slain, when there is a screech from the platform in front of you. 'Sacrilege! Seize the thief!' Sige is pointing at you, her body trembling with rage. Madhaerios is staring open-mouthed at the locket. Dunyazad cries: 'It is the relic of which Carolina spoke on her death-bed – the Fate of Rangor.' Sige cuts her short with an imperious gesture. 'Guards! Luthaur! Kill this treacherous dog.' If you try to open the locket, turn to **376**. If you draw your sword and try to fight off the guards, turn to **399**.

111

By now a small crowd of townsfolk has gathered to watch the spectacle. From behind you comes a creaking noise, followed by a yawning crash. You turn in time to see the roof of the inn collapse, sending up a cascade of swirling sparks. You are just wondering where you are going to spend the night when you feel the light touch of metal against your neck, and a gruff voice whispers, 'One move and you're a cut of beef, stranger.' Out of the frying pan and into the fire! If you stay still as the voice advises, turn to **341**. If you wish to act, you may shout for help (turn to **200**) or try to disarm him (turn to **292**).

112

You follow him stealthily as he makes his way out of the bowl, to a crystal chariot waiting near by. It is drawn by two Ectovults and driven by a small Crystal Sprite, who bows humbly as his master climbs into the chariot. Then they are off. You try to keep up with them, but the chariot is too fast for you. Soon you are left alone and lost in the desolate crystal wastes. Your adventure ends here.

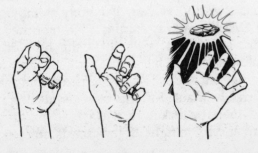

113

It is time to flee, but your horse beats you to it. She rears violently, throwing you to the ground, and then bolts. You fall awkwardly and feel your left leg crumple beneath you. You try to stand up, and the pain hits home. You black out for a moment. When you open your eyes once more, black sparks are dancing before them. A deafening drone surrounds you. Then the pain comes once more. Turn to **336**.

114

You feel a soft weight drop upon your shoulder. You turn your head to find yourself staring into the eyes of a serpent. You shudder and automatically grab for it. But it is too fast for you. In an instant its thick coils are wrapped around your neck. 'Meet Caduceus,' says the woman. Turn to **307**.

115

The creature appears in a shimmering haze, but rapidly scuttles towards you. Your eyes ache simply from looking at its foul, ulcerous body. Its single claw clacks repeatedly against its slimy carapace and, with each movement it makes, a new tide of nausea sweeps over you. Remembering Enthymesis's words, you blow a shrill blast on the whistle. The creature flinches, but continues to advance slowly. You will have to battle it while blowing as hard as you can on the whistle!

MAIJEM-NOSOTH   SKILL 10   STAMINA 10

If you do not have your sword, you fight at −2, and may not strike *killing blows*. If you defeat the creature, turn to **316**.

116

You make your way through the shifting mists, treading carefully on the slippery ground beneath your feet. As you walk, you notice shapes moving beneath the translucent surface. The mist muffles sound, but a screeching whistle penetrates. *Test your Luck.* If you are Lucky, turn to **193**. If you are Unlucky, turn to **209**.

117

As you charge up the stairs towards him, he looses off a crossbow bolt at you. At this range he can hardly miss, but you throw yourself against the wall in an attempt to dodge. The bolt catches you in the side and you wheel backwards, gripping it. The pain doubles you up and you lose your balance, slipping from the steps. You land on the packed dirt of the courtyard, the impact driving the bolt deep into you. Your adventure ends here.

118

The crossbow bolt thuds into the palace guard, and with a shriek he tumbles from the walkway down into the courtyard. You are just congratulating yourself on your accuracy when you hear shouting from the guard tower opposite the keep. A troop of guards pile out and begin to search the area. You are quickly spotted and overwhelmed by them. Turn to 355.

119

While searching through the palace you have inherited, you come upon a scrying mirror, set into a wall of crystal. A Servant shuffles forward and shows you how to use it; you train it on Kallamehr, hoping to see the fruits of your sacrifice. Sure enough, the fields are full of villagers once more. Yet a shadow still hangs over the land. As you focus it on Kallamehr's palace, you see Sige the Silent being invested as the new Lord of Kallamehr. She is aware of your gaze, for she stares back at you and sneers. 'The Abyss may be yours,' she whispers, 'but Kallamehr is mine, now and for ever!' It seems you have saved Kallamehr's people, only to abandon them to a dark tyrant.

120

You must now fight the other two Elves.

	SKILL	STAMINA
Second BLACK ELF	7	6
Third BLACK ELF	7	6

Fight both the Elves at the same time. Each will make a separate attack on you during each Attack Round, but you must choose which of the two you will fight. Fight your nominated target as in a normal battle. Against the other, throw the dice for your Attack Strength in the normal way, but you will not wound it if your Attack Strength is greater; you will just have parried its blow. Of course, if its Attack Strength is greater, it will have wounded you in the normal way. If you defeat the Elves, turn to **311**.

121

Looking down the street you see a pair of rough-looking peasants who seem to be gazing at you rather intently. As you approach them, you notice that their awed gaze is not directed *at you*, but at something *behind you*. You twist round in your saddle, to find yourself staring at a silent line of men and women in the robes of priests. You turn to spur your horse on, but another line of priests has appeared ahead of you, and one snatches the reins from your hand. There is nothing you can do. The priests close in and raise their clubs. Turn to **239**.

122

The Troll looks round cautiously as you approach, waiting for you to act. He doesn't seem hostile; he is more concerned with rooting out whatever he has trapped in the hole. He hasn't had much success yet, probably because his tiny brain hasn't thought of stripping the branches from the sapling, so it keeps catching on the edges of the hole. If you attack him, turn to **6**. If you suggest he strips the leaves off his tree, turn to **345**.

123

The way forward begins to slope downwards, and the forest floor beneath your feet starts to soften. Soon you are squelching through boggy ground, with mud sucking at your shins. Flies begin to home in on you, and the heat saps your strength. Lose 1 point of STAMINA. After an hour's painful progress, the ground rises and the track you are on meets another. There is nothing to distinguish this part of the forest from the others you have been through, but you must choose whether to go along the new track to the left or the right. If you go right, turn to **132**. If you go left, turn to **231**.

124

You are some way up the immense chain when you lose your grip, slithering and sliding down it, then falling to the hard crystal below. The number you rolled is the number of STAMINA points you lose. If you wish to try again, roll one die. If the result is a 6, turn to **219**. If the result is 1–5, lose that number of

STAMINA points and choose again. If you would prefer to investigate the creaking sound, turn to **237**.

When you reach the village's stockade the army is no longer visible, but you know that it is only a matter of time before it will sweep over this settlement. Strangely, the gates are shut when you arrive, so you leap from your horse and hammer on them, bellowing to be let in. You look up in time to see a face staring down at you, but it pulls back when you catch its eye. A quavering voice from behind the palisade tells you to leave. You try to explain to the frightened villagers that they must flee, but in vain. Even as you speak, the black horde is darkening the hilltop in the distance. You abandon the villagers to their fate and ride on. Turn to **53**.

126

You abandon the wretch to his fate and turn back to climb the dark flight of steps. As you set foot on the first stair, you hear a faint pattering behind you. You turn to see what it is, but you are too late to avoid the blow. Turn to **355**.

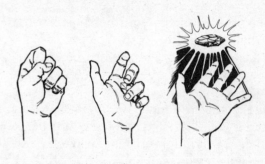

127

Gulping in a lungful of air, you reach down and grasp the bars, then pull yourself under, until you can kick with your feet. There is a small gap between the bars and the bed of the river, through which you will be able to swim. The water is faintly illuminated by the torchlight up above, and as you edge through the gap you notice that the river-bed is littered with countless treasures. Your attention is caught by a jewel-encrusted sword, its pommel an enormous blue gem which pulses with an inner light. If you swim down to grab the sword, turn to **247**. If you carry on under the bars, turn to **377**.

128

You slip into one of the buildings near by and try to find some clue to explain the mystery of the abandoned village. You quickly realize that you have entered the house of a wizard or herbalist. Fragrant drying herbs, arcane books and scrolls, and vials of coloured liquids litter a desk in the corner to your right. To your left sits a rune-carved table, on which lies a half-eaten knuckle of cured ham. Across the far wall you see a row of puppets, dangling on their strings from a high shelf above a cupboard. If you go to look at them, turn to **244**. If you examine the wizard's paraphernalia, turn to **333**.

129

You spur your tired horse through the familiar countryside of Kallamehr province, pausing only briefly at watering-holes and resisting the temptation to stop and warn everyone you pass. On and on you ride, until your mare begins to stumble and you know she can go on no further. You must have rest if you are to reach Kallamehr. You are almost falling out of your saddle as you ride into Kamadan, an affluent market-town. An ostler helps you from your horse and you lurch into the inn. With barely a grunt at the innkeeper, you stagger up the stairs and into the nearest room. You collapse, exhausted, on the rickety bed. If you have Sige's pomander, turn to **44**. If not, turn to **9**.

130

You trudge wearily down to the rooming-house you were staying at before you left Kallamehr. What happened to Lady Carolina? One minute you were on a life-and-death mission to save the city, the next you were virtually ignored. You spend a frustrating night in the seedy rooming-house, turning these matters over in your mind. Tick off a time box. Next morning you return to the palace, to find that you are not the only one who wishes to enter – a column of citizens is filing sombrely through the gates. You join them, listening to their speculation as to the cause of Carolina's sudden demise. Some say it was grief at the horrific death of her husband, while others claim that dark powers were responsible. You enter the courtyard and see the body lying in state, flanked by guards. On a platform behind the catafalque sit Madhaerios, Dunyazad of Ikhtiyan, Asiah Albudur and Sige the Silent. Turn to **344**.

131

If you have any remaining potions labelled 'Arahl', 'Zazzaz' and 'Ghulsh', you may add any or all of them to the brew. Make a note of which potions you add. If you wait to see what happens now, turn to **68**. If you wish to drink the brew, turn to **45**.

132

The track you are on winds slowly upwards, and you begin to tire of the endless foot-slogging. Lose 1 point of STAMINA. Finally you emerge from the trees on to a grassy knoll which peeps out above the forest. Sitting down for a brief rest, you survey the featureless forest canopy below which stretches as far as you can see in every direction. Two other paths lead back into the forest from the knoll. You may take the one which leads towards the sun (turn to 231), or the other, darker route (turn to 312).

133

The path follows the river downstream for some way before turning into the trees. Very soon you are back at the glade with the mighty oak, and pleased to see your horse still safely tethered, munching contentedly at the grass. You mount up and spur her along the path and out of the forest, glad to be away from the trees and their treacherous pathways. After several minutes, you look back and are astonished to see a sparkling blue lake where the forest should be. Far off, in its midst, a tiny hut rises above the waters, supported by its familiar spindly legs. Aletheia has many ways of discouraging unwelcome visitors to her realm, it seems. Now you have a weapon, it is time to confront the vast horde . . . alone. Turn to 325.

134

Whatever you give Barolo, cross it off your *Adventure Sheet*. Barolo thanks you for your gift, and wishes you good luck in your mission. You wave him goodbye and ride off. Tick off a time box and turn to **290**.

135

The Anemorus is black and obscenely blubbery. Though limbless, it has a powerful tail which it uses to push itself towards you. A writhing mass of pinkish tentacles sits where its head should be. If you do not have your sword, turn to **184**. Otherwise you must fight the Anemorus.

ANEMORUS   SKILL 5   STAMINA 10

If you kill the Anemorus, turn to **357**.

136

Your journey continues once more, as you attempt to make up some of the time you have lost. If you decide to cut across country, turn to **287**. If you stick to the roads, turn to **256**.

137

You slip into the stables. The horses stir uneasily, but you whisper gently to them and they soon quieten. Making yourself comfortable in a pile of straw, you await the dawn. Tick off a time box and turn to **276**.

138

Have you lit your Jheera torch yet? If so, turn to **199**. If not, turn to **171**.

139

Shaken by your experience, you return to your horse. Soon you are riding once more through the woodland. Tick off a time box. The road begins to slope downwards, and you wend your way along its many curves until you are following the banks of a fast-flowing stream. The sun is lowering in the sky behind you, and the air is alive with the noises of insects. Ahead of you is a crude stockade. You ride in and are quickly surrounded by a dozen curious villagers. They seem much friendlier than most others you have encountered so far, and you begin to hope that you will be treated hospitably here. Sure enough, you are invited inside for a meal and a drink (restore up to 4 STAMINA points). Soon you are relaxing in the pleasant company of these simple folk. After a while you hear a commotion from outside your hut, and several villagers slip out. If you follow them outside, turn to **66**. If you stay with your hosts in the hut, turn to **385**.

140

You are led straight down to the stables to choose your horse. While you are preparing to leave, tall Sige approaches. Her voice is low, almost inaudible, and you understand how she came to be called 'the Silent'. She tells you that she has a valuable magical item which will aid you on your journey and bring you the luck of the gods. It is a pomander of rare herbs – if worn around your neck it will also remove your need for sleep. It is passed up to you by Sige's servant, a poor deformed creature who shuffles slowly and wears a hood, no doubt to hide his piteously ugly face. Sige quietly wishes you a safe and fruitful journey. Bundling together your possessions, you hurry into the bustling courtyard. With no time for ceremony, you mount your steed and pick your way through the crowd to the gate. A swift ride along the Way of Flint brings you to Kallamehr's Grand Gate. Turn to **329**.

141

'Most kind!' says Bythos, reaching out to take the Golden Fist. He tosses it over his shoulder, then draws in a deep breath. Before you can act, a freezing blast strikes you, and crystals form on your skin. They quickly melt, however, and Bythos advances on you. If you flee, turn to **335**. If you would rather attack, turn to **149**.

142

You wade through the wine towards the spot where the body fell. As you peer down into the murky depths an arm shoots up from the wine and grabs your leg. Caught off balance, you tumble head first into the dark liquid. A moment later the creature is on top of you, its hands grabbing your shoulders and forcing you down. The wine closes over your head. Roll two dice. If the result is *less than* your STAMINA, turn to **391**. If the result is *greater than or equal to* your STAMINA, turn to **107**.

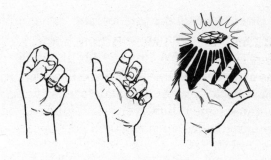

143

Luthaur is fighting with a wickedly barbed scimitar, its blade darkened. As it slices into your flesh, you feel a stinging sensation which begins rapidly to spread. Luthaur's sword is envenomed – hardly the action of a hero. As the poison takes hold and you topple off the platform, you spit a last, defiant curse at the treacherous rat who has killed you. Your adventure ends here.

144

You snatch up the extinguished Jheera torch and set about relighting it. It is smouldering once more as the first hornets gather in the entrance to the cave. You rush to the back of the cave and watch as the cloud swarms towards you. For a moment you fear that the smoke is not harming the hornets; then they begin to fall. Soon the cave floor is littered with dead and dying bodies. When you are certain that it is safe once more, you ride out and down towards the horde. Turn to **235**.

145

You sit and stare at the hut, looking for signs of life. There is a heat-haze around you, and you realize how much your trek through the forest has tired you. If you have Sige's pomander, turn to **152**. Otherwise turn to **29**.

146

You drag yourself away from the tentacles and clamber up on to the crystal . . . only to find yourself facing the creature you saw land earlier. Turn to **135**.

147

You wind back the crossbow's string and fit a bolt. Taking careful aim, you shoot. You are rewarded by a howl of pain from the Troll, and he glares at you from across the river. Before you have an opportunity to shoot again, though, he has crashed off into the undergrowth. Turn to **381**.

148
A black shadow hovers above you – but before you can focus on it you hear a high-pitched scream which changes to a gurgle, and sticky grey slime spatters your face. Pain grips you by the head, and you lose your grip on the window-sill. There is a ghastly snap as you land, but the acid on your face has already done its foul work. Your adventure ends here.

149
Bythos takes a step back in amazement. 'Gatherer! What treason is this?' he bellows. The door behind you opens and cowled figures pour into the room. You draw your sword but have no opportunity to use it. Skeletal Servants of Bythos overwhelm you and hold you before their master. Turn to **313**.

150
You drag the bodies of the guardsmen into the nearby ditch and stride into the palace courtyard. The first person you meet is a footman; he is laden down by the weight of a heavy chest he is carrying and is hurrying towards the stables. When he sees you, he hails you and demands to know your business. You tell him you have an urgent message for Lady Dunyazad. He directs you to an antechamber

and promises to fetch the noblewoman. As the footman scurries off, you make your way into the antechamber and wait. Turn to **310**.

151

You slip down the rope to the courtyard and, keeping in the shadows around its edge, begin to make your way back to the servants' quarters. You notice a guardsman marching along the walkway on the walls. If you had remained on the roof of the keep he would probably have spotted you. Turn to **204**.

152

Soon you become too impatient to wait any longer. You can hear faint movements from within the hut, but nothing more happens. You call out, but if there is anyone within the hut they are ignoring you. You will have to take the initiative. If you walk under the hut, turn to **254**. If you climb up one of the legs, turn to **202**.

153

You dig your feet into the flanks of your unwilling mare, and she trots down the slope. The nearer you get to the mass below, the more you are struck by its sheer size. The rank smell hangs heavy, almost physically repelling you. If Mema is with you, turn to **283**. If not, turn to **306**.

154

The Gatherer stops his chanting when he sees you and stoops to pick up a small shard of crystal with a skeletal hand. He takes each end and pulls it out until he holds a ragged crystal javelin, which he then hurls at you. Turn to **105**.

155

Your walk to the nearest village takes you the better part of an afternoon. By now, you think to yourself, whoever was sent to scout to the east will be leagues ahead of you – even though you left Kallamehr before them. When you finally reach the settlement, you are treated with respect. The village elder recognizes the seal on the scroll you bear and is quick to furnish you with the fastest horse in the village. Soon you are thundering along the road, trying to make up some of the time you lost. The sun is half way below the rim of the world, and shadows streak the greying lands around you, when you see a dark bundle lying on the road ahead. If you ignore it and continue at a gallop, turn to **301**. If you stop to examine it, turn to **249**.

156

'But I might wake her!' Asiah replies to your suggestion. Everyone stares at her, incredulous. 'Very well. I'm not one to spoil a ceremony.' She goes across to Carolina, gives her an affectionate peck, then smooths the dead ruler's hair from her brow. 'It's time to wake up, dear,' she says. But for the nervous shuffling of feet, the courtyard is silent. Dunyazad turns to the guards and says quietly, 'Arrest the presumptuous dog.' Before you can defend yourself they are upon you. Turn to **355**.

157

You steel yourself and leap through. You feel no heat, and realize that the wall was merely an illusion. You land in a cramped chamber, surprising four silver-skinned humanoids. They are Murkurons, well armed and equipped for adventuring. As you burst into the room, three of them are struggling with a small iron-bound door, while the fourth is standing near by. If you attack immediately, turn to **195**. If you wait for them to react, turn to **253**.

158

You glance through the books and scrolls, but the rambling text means nothing to you. The vials look more promising. Though many are cracked and their contents spilt, a few remain intact. Of these you salvage the three which seem the least noxious, each containing an unexciting, cloudy, brown liquid. Each is labelled in the same crabbed handwriting. You may risk drinking one or more of the liquids now, or you may take any or all of them with you. If you decide to take them with you, note down the name of each potion you take on your *Adventure Sheet*, together with the paragraph number which you should go to if you decide to drink it. You may drink one of these potions at any time that you would normally be able to drink a potion (that is, as long as you are not in battle). Remember: note down the number of the paragraph you are at *before* turning to the relevant paragraph for the potion you are about to drink; you should also make a note of the fact when you have drunk that potion. Each vial contains only *one* mouthful – so, once you have drunk a potion, it has all gone.

If you drink the potion marked 'Ghulsh'	Turn to **258**
If you drink the potion marked 'Arahl'	Turn to **285**
If you drink the potion marked 'Zazzaz'	Turn to **369**

Once you have finished checking the potions, turn to **270**.

159

You kiss Carolina's hand respectfully and join the growing crowd lining the walls of the courtyard. You wait for several hours as the well-wishers pay their last respects. Finally servants come forward and place the lid on the coffin. Madhaerios steps forward nervously and addresses the crowd. Solemnly, he reads the service for the burial of the dead. After a few minutes' silence, he speaks again, reassuring the crowd of the safety of Kallamehr; he talks of the execution of traitors, and the successes of the army against Bei-Han. Finally he announces that since Carolina left no legitimate heir, he will be assuming the title of Baron himself. The ceremony over, the nobles return once more to their quarters, and the courtyard empties. Downcast by the funeral, you contemplate your next course of action. If you wish to leave Kallamehr, turn to **183**. If you decide to stay and continue your investigations, turn to **252**.

160

The old crone lets out a grating screech and drops to her knees. 'We are lost! We shall all die! Abandoned by our saviour!' As you turn to leave, the villagers close in around you, pleading desperately. When you brush them aside, their pleas turn to threats. Several are carrying rusty farm tools and begin to menace you with them. If you wish to attack the villagers, turn to **191**. If you surrender to their wishes, turn to **208**.

161

As you draw your sword, Bythos roars, 'Treachery!' and draws in a deep breath. You leap to strike him, hoping that his huge size will give you a chance to strike first. But luck is not with you. He breathes a freezing blast at you, and crystals form with startling speed on your skin. As Bythos continues to breathe at you the crystals spread, and soon you are encased, a living statue, doomed to live out the rest of your life as a morbid ornament for the Master of the Abyss.

162

You cross to the barred trapdoor. It has a lock on it but, when you grasp the bars, you find it has been left unlocked. You lift it easily with both hands and reach through to see whether you can grasp the man's hand. Unfortunately he is too far away, so you call to him to edge closer. From his muscular build, you guess that this is Ramedes the Invincible, Lady Carolina's champion. He starts to make painful progress towards you, one hand at a time. Then you are aware of somebody behind you – just as they kick you violently in the back, sending you headlong into the gurgling darkness. Turn to **175**.

163

The rest of the night passes uneventfully, and with the morning you resume your journey. The leagues stretch on, and you see a range of mountains in the distance ahead of you. You pass through several villages, and are surprised at the surly reactions of the villagers. As you pass them you hear them muttering under their breath, and when you stop to refill your water-bottle, they do their best to ignore you. The sun is low in the sky when you enter the small town of Hasrah, in which lies the Temple of Fourga. You could travel a few more hours if you wished, but you would have to spend another night in the open. Tick off a time box. If you ride on, turn to **26**. If you seek hospitality at the Temple of Fourga, turn to **4**.

164

You walk across the crystal wastes until you come upon a huge metal ring embedded in the ground. From it, a chain with links as thick as your body rises into the air, up into the clouds from which a desolate moaning is coming. It would be difficult, but you could climb the chain (turn to 294). Alternatively, you could investigate the creaking sound, which is still faintly audible (turn to 237).

165

You return to your quarters and spend the rest of the night on your uncomfortable straw pallet. Next morning, a palace guardsman bursts into your quarters and demands that you follow him. He leads you to the antechamber and ushers you in. No sooner have you walked past him than the pommel of his sword descends on the back of your head, and you crumple to the ground. Turn to 355.

166

You search the bodies of the Ogre and the Goblin, but they possess nothing but a few revolting morsels of meat. You carry on down the path some distance, noticing the huge clumps of foxgloves which grow on your right. After a while you come across a path which turns off to the right. If you have three numbers written down on your *Adventure Sheet*, turn to the paragraph they indicate. Otherwise, if you go down the path to the right, write the number '3' after any other numbers on your *Adventure Sheet* and turn to **268**. If you carry straight on, write the number '1' after any other numbers on your *Adventure Sheet* and turn to **17**. If you already have one of these numbers written down, you should choose the other option.

167

You cast about the smoke-filled room for an alternative escape route. *Test your Luck*. If you are Lucky, turn to **392**. If you are Unlucky, turn to **323**.

168

As one, the Crystal Warriors close in and raise their hammers . . . weaponless, you resign yourself to your fate. Your adventure ends here.

169

As Luthaur's body topples off the platform, you sheathe your sword and turn to the four nobles, now flanked by guards. 'I act not as a traitor,' you say, 'but as a loyal servant of the House of Rangor.' You explain that someone has deliberately tried to prevent you from passing on the news of the impending invasion – someone who must be in league with the invaders! If you wish to accuse one of the nobles of treachery, turn to **334**. If you have the Sealed Locket and wish to explain how you came by it, turn to **320**.

170

You draw some water from the village well and use it to clean the sticky mire off Mema. Make a note of this. Tick off a time box, then turn to **396**.

171

The black cloud is advancing on you with terrifying speed. You fumble with your tinder-box, cursing your clumsy fingers. *Test your Luck*. If you are Lucky, turn to **217**. If you are Unlucky, turn to **284**.

172

The creature tries to slither away between your legs, but you grasp it and force it down by sitting on its back. Although it is slippery, and you are blinded, you manage to get a firm grip around its neck. You are about to bang its head on the floor when it begins to sob. You pause a moment while your vision clears, revealing the pathetic figure of a young girl, coated from head to foot in foul-smelling green slime. Cautiously you release your grasp and pick up the slender blow-pipe she used to puff the blinding dust at you. Pocketing it, you ask the girl her name. Turn to **315**.

173

You take a step towards the silver creature, and he shakes his head sadly. Flame gouts from his out-stretched arms, and you are engulfed in fire. These flames, however, are real . . .

174

You are blinded by the sunlight which streams in through the window. The bustle of the market below filters into the room. You are bathed in sweat and trembling uncontrollably, the ghastly image still lingering in your mind. Was it a premonition, or just your fear ruling your imagination? Your thoughts are interrupted by a call from Bedrah, one of your fellow adventurers. Buckling on your sword, you follow her to Lady Carolina's audience-chamber to decide which of you will be the volunteers. Although you had intended to stay and defend the city, you may still volunteer if you wish to change your mind. Will you:

Ride north for the army?	Turn to **92**
Scout to the east?	Turn to **104**
Stay behind after all?	Turn to **182**

175

You land painfully on the soft floor of the pit. To one side you can make out a single luminous eye regarding you from amid a bulky, shifting mass of mottled grey flesh. Beneath the eye is a gaping black maw, from which come ghastly sucking noises. It is a Quagrant, a horror bred by only the most loathsome and warped sorcerers. You have only a moment in which to act. Will you:

Use a blow-pipe, if you have one which has not been used?	Turn to **378**
Use the Spitting Fly, if you know it?	Turn to **328**
Fight the horror with your sword?	Turn to **314**
Flee up the rough walls of the pit?	Turn to **18**

176

You eventually find a small furry creature hiding beneath a rotting log. While it is still startled, you whisk it into your backpack and hurry back to the hut, which you find with surprising ease. Back inside, the woman greets you quite pleasantly, introduces her serpent Caduceus to you, and tells you that her name is Aletheia. Caduceus swallows your gift whole and wraps himself affectionately round your shoulders, while Aletheia tells you a little about him. Turn to 307.

177

Cross 1 set of Provisions and 4 Gold Pieces off your *Adventure Sheet*. Tasbadh greedily gulps down the food you give him and pockets the coins. With a loud belch, he says, 'Right, let's get our heads down for the night,' and commandeers your blanket which you had draped over the horse behind you. 'Better make a fire to keep the beasts away!' he says, settling himself down in your warm blanket. You spend a cold night, tending the fire and listening to Tasbadh's mighty snoring. The next morning, Tasbadh seems a little better, but urgently he reminds you of the Death Spell which is squeezing the life from him. Soon you are on your way to Gebaan. No sooner have you ridden into the village than Tasbadh springs off your steed and hurries away into a large building. You notice a lurid sign outside: 'The Purple Poignard'. Surely the Healer doesn't live in a tavern? Tick off a time box. If you have the Golden Fist, turn to **121**. If not, turn to **109**.

178

Your opponent seems to anticipate your move, and dodges back behind you. The blade of his knife pricks your jugular. Across the way a group of townsfolk are staring at you expectantly. Turn to **200**.

179

You race down to the chariot, brandishing your sword wildly. The Crystal Sprite spots you and flees. Leaping on to the chariot, you grab the reins and yell at the Ectovults to move. They ignore you. All your efforts to get the chariot moving are in vain. You are stranded, alone in the crystal wastes. Your adventure ends here.

180

The Troll soon disappears off into the undergrowth, still dragging the sapling behind it. You splash your face with the river water and prepare to carry on, refreshed by your rest. Turn to 381.

181

You are still locked in battle with the Caveman as the first hornets swarm into the cave. You launch a kick at the primitive creature, then dive for the Jheera torch. You are too late. The torch has gone out, and the Caveman is too stupid to recognize the threat of the hornets. His bone crashes on your head.

182

'How much for that one?' says the greasy-haired peasant, pointing at a rust-coated sword on a market stall. 'Wot, this?' replies the stallholder, pulling it from a jumbled pile. 'More 'n you can afford, matey. This 'un's not for sticking your pigs with. Fangthane steel, this. Pulled it from the ruins of Kallamehr meself, I did, a few years back. Last a

Turn of Turns, it will, which is more 'n could be said for its last owner. Wot a mess they was!' Many years have passed since the fall of Kallamehr. You shared the fate which overwhelmed it. Your remains lie unmourned among the rubble and debris.

183

You waste no time in retrieving your horse and setting out from the city. You ride east along the same route you used those few fateful days earlier. Tick off a time box. If you have heard of Enthymesis and wish to search for him, turn to 5. Otherwise, turn to 325.

184

Your blows are useless against the blubbery, tentacled thing. It closes its grip on you, and you are engulfed by the writhing mass – to be slowly digested by the creature.

185

The guards chuckle with glee and pocket the money. One of them leads you through the gates and into a small antechamber. 'I'll fetch someone who can help,' he says and slips out of the room. You wait for a while. Turn to 310.

186

You hurriedly wind back the string of the bow and snap in a bolt. You must shoot the jailer before he sees what you are up to. Roll two dice. If the result is *less than* your SKILL, turn to **227**. If the result is *greater than or equal to* your SKILL, turn to **240**.

187

You step over the slimy green corpses and take the opportunity to examine the objects you have picked up: a set of priceless gems, shaped like eyes, and a jewelled tiara. To your experienced gaze they look magical, so you stow them in your pack and make your way along the passage. Soon it leads into a round chamber. Turn to **82**.

188

You take the black-clad figure by surprise, and it splutters as you catch it full on the chest. You must fight the Winged Assassin for three rounds. Remember, you may not score a *killing blow* on it; you are weak from lack of rest, so reduce your SKILL by 2 points.

WINGED ASSASSIN   SKILL 5   STAMINA 10

If you are still alive at the end of three rounds, turn to **79**.

The missile speeds straight at you, but too low, and passes harmlessly between your legs. There is a strangled yelp from behind you, and you turn to see a Goblin with sword raised, staring in surprise at the bolt, which is protruding from his belly. 'Nice shooting, Gok. Next time *I* use the crossbow,' he croaks, and topples backwards. The Goblin who fired the crossbow flings it guiltily aside and draws a small knife from his belt. He charges towards you with a curse, and you prepare for battle. But after three steps he is whipped off his feet and yanked violently upwards by a noose-trap. 'Got 'im!' says a voice near by, and yet another Goblin comes into view, holding the other end of the rope. When he sees you, his jaw drops and he lets go of the rope, dropping his accomplice in a heap and fleeing. You chuckle to yourself and advance up the path, marvelling at the Goblins' incompetence. A little further on, you hear more Goblin voices ahead. 'Don't worry Gublb, *I'll* pulp 'im,' says a squeaky voice. You saunter confidently round a bend in the path, only to find yourself facing an *enormous* Ogre, his tiny Goblin-sized head glaring furiously at you. Behind him cowers the Goblin you encountered earlier.

	SKILL	STAMINA
OGRE	10	12
GOBLIN	5	4

Fight them one at a time, the Ogre first. If you defeat them both, turn to **166**.

190

Your sword flashes towards the Gatherer and impales him through the chest. He leans forward and grasps its pommel, then pulls it from him with a grating noise, as of metal on bone. Then he raises it and charges at you. The last thing you see are the skeletal features beneath his cowl.

191

The villagers are not trained warriors, and two fall straight away to your assault. Behind them, three more block your path with their sickles.

	SKILL	STAMINA
First VILLAGER	4	3
Second VILLAGER	3	3

Fight the first two villagers simultaneously. Each will have a separate attack on you during each Attack Round, but you must choose at the beginning of each Attack Round which of the two you will fight. Attack your chosen target as in a normal battle. Against the other, throw for your Attack Strength in the normal way, but you will not wound him if your Attack Strength is greater; you will have merely parried his blow. If his Attack Strength is greater, he will have wounded you in the normal way. If you defeat the first two villagers, a third still bars your way to your horse.

Third VILLAGER   SKILL 3   STAMINA 3

If you win, turn to **347**.

192

As your horse falls forward, you leap from the saddle, but your foot tangles in the stirrup and you are dashed to the ground. Lose 2 STAMINA points. You stagger to your feet and are dismayed to find that the proud mare you chose is now lamed. You cannot continue your journey on her, but must search for a village to get a new horse. Turn to **155**.

193

A silvery shape shoots past your head and crashes into the ground, shattering into a million milky droplets. These re-form into a grotesque winged reptile, its limbless translucent body pulsing with unnatural energy. A vicious beak protrudes from its bulbous head, and milky eyes full of malice peer balefully around. The Ectovult flounders about until it bumps into a silver chalice, which it greedily consumes. The winged horror then flies off with the chalice still visible, quivering inside its body. If you have a crossbow and wish to shoot the Ectovult, turn to **271**. Otherwise, turn to **322**.

194

While you are writhing from the effects of the dust, you hear the door of the house slam, and running footsteps fading away. When your vision finally returns, you see the empty cupboard in front of you, sticky green footmarks leading out of it. If you have not yet searched the desk in the corner and wish to do so, turn to **158**. Otherwise you may follow the footsteps, (turn to **206**).

195

You cut down the first Murkuron on the spot, and prepare to battle the remaining three. They look round fearfully, but remain braced against the door. Too late, you realize they were trying to hold the door shut rather than open it. Seconds later, the door gives way and squat, scaly creatures flood in. The Kokomokoa swarm all over the Murkurons, and four charge at you.

	SKILL	STAMINA
First KOKOMOKOA	6	5
Second KOKOMOKOA	5	5
Third KOKOMOKOA	5	6
Fourth KOKOMOKOA	5	5

You must fight the Kokomokoa one at a time. Remember: if you do not have your sword, your Attack is at −2, and you may not score *killing blows*. If you defeat them, turn to **370**.

196

Your sword is too small to use against Bythos, so you may not strike *killing blows*. If you have Barolo's buckler it too is useless, so you will lose its SKILL bonus.

BYTHOS   SKILL 10   STAMINA 10

If you defeat Bythos, turn to **291**.

197

You point Mema's slender tube up at the jailer and blow hard. A cloud of black powder shoots into the air, and then descends on you. Soon you are coughing and choking, and the laughter of the jailer from up above does little to ease your discomfort. Turn to **352**.

198

You explain to the guard that you couldn't sleep, and that you fancied some fresh air and the view from the battlements. He eyes you suspiciously and tells you that only palace guardsmen are allowed on to the battlements. You apologize profusely and return to the courtyard, knowing that he is watching you all the way. Turn to **165**.

199

The cloud of black hornets swirls round you, and you curse as the breeze picks up, dissipating the Jheera smoke. The hornets are closing in on you. If you flee back up the hillside, turn to **386**. If you make for the river which runs along the valley to your right, turn to **42**. If you make for the cave entrance you passed, turn to **106**.

200

You cry out in alarm, but the townsfolk just point at you and laugh. 'So that's the way a hero gets to be famous nowadays, is it?' asks the gruff voice, and you suddenly recognize it as that of Barolo, your old blade-master. He spins you round and pockets his knife. You notice that he now has a wooden left leg, but he makes no mention of it. 'You'd best come and stay with me,' he suggests. Turn to **375**.

201

One of the Crystal Warriors strides in your direction and swings its hammer. You try to defend yourself with your sword, but it glances harmlessly off the warrior. If you have an onyx sceptre or a golden fist, and wish to use it as a makeshift club, turn to **62**. If you wish to grapple the warrior, turn to **305**.

202

You shin up the nearest leg until you find yourself clinging close to the bottom of the hut. Looking along the base, you can make out an opening set in the middle. The only way to reach it is to grab the supporting beams and swing your way into it, legs first. You look down at the ground, which seems even further away than you had imagined. Roll two dice. If the result is *less than* your SKILL, turn to 337. If the result is *greater than or equal to* your SKILL, turn to 229.

203

Before long, you chance upon a host of crystal statues, their serried ranks stretching away into the mist. Looking closer, you see that each is a human entombed within a crystal shell. If you bear the wound which changes colour, turn to 52. Otherwise, turn to 75.

204

Suddenly you hear the sound of grating metal near by. Behind you is a small metal door which leads into one of the outbuildings of the palace. A key is turning in the lock. You flatten yourself against the wall by the side of the door. It is flung outward, nearly crushing you. From your hiding-place behind the door you hear several voices. You recognize one as that of Luthaur, the traitorous adventurer who embarrassed you in front of Dunyazad. 'Put up quite a struggle, eh, lads?' he says. 'Yes, Luthaur, they don't call him Ramedes the Invincible for nothing – even with enough brew inside him to drop a dragon, he fought like a dozen men.' 'Don't worry, the other one'll be a lot easier.'

Do they mean you? The voices reach the other end of the courtyard and you hear a door slam. For some reason, they've left this door open. If you creep cautiously down the passage the men came out of, turn to **363**. If you slip back to your pallet in the servants' quarters, turn to **165**. If you wish to spend the rest of the night hidden in the stables, turn to **137**.

205

You feel a tremendous pressure as your body crumples. The palace fades from view and you lose consciousness. You awaken in a rice paddy. There is nobody about, so you wade to the nearest path and make your way along it. It leads to a village, but this village, like the others you came across earlier in your wanderings, is deserted. You hurry on through Kallamehr, passing through more deserted settlements. When you arrive at Kallamehr, you realize the extent of your failure. You have defeated Bythos, but Kallamehr has lost almost all of its people. You may have saved your own skin, but at the cost of thousands of innocent people. You are no hero.

206

Outside the building, the sticky patches lead along the main street towards the far gate. You fetch your horse and mount up. Unfortunately the trail gets fainter and fainter as it goes on and, by the time you reach the gate, the footsteps are barely visible in the dust. You realize that your quarry has eluded you.

Disappointed, you continue your journey. Turn to **22**.

207
You wrest the sapling from the Troll's dead fingers, and start tearing off the leaves and stuffing them in your backpack. Once you have stripped the tree, you head back to the river, finding yourself on a trail which runs along the bank. Turn to **133**.

208
A ragged cheer goes up from the villagers as you give your assent. You are led back to the hut, and more food is brought. The old woman advises you to prepare for the test which awaits you, but she seems unable to explain its nature. The more she speaks to you, the madder she seems, and you begin to doubt her prophecy. But who are you to complain? You settle back to rest, staring up through the smoke-hole at the bright moon. Turn to **319**.

209
How many of the following items do you possess: eye-shaped gems, jewelled tiara, gem-encrusted breastplate, feather boots, golden fist, pearl-inlaid skull, onyx sceptre, crystal globe? If you have *fewer than* four, turn to **351**. If you have four or more, turn to **393**.

210

The guards are taken aback when they find themselves staring at the blade of your sword. They look
at each other briefly, then one shouts, 'Get 'im!' If
you have Sige's pomander and are still wearing it,
turn to **83**. Otherwise, turn to **242**.

211

As you watch, the ant-covered hand grabs a stick
which was lying near by. It then withdraws back
into the hole, and you hear scraping noises coming
from within. You are not entirely sure what is going
on within the mound, but you are glad that you
didn't get involved. Turn to **58**.

212

You walk slowly up to the chariot and climb in,
while the Crystal Sprite bows reverently. Then he
lets out a high-pitched yell, and the Ectovults lurch
off. Soon you are skimming across the plain at
breathtaking speed. A few minutes later, the spires
of a fantastic crystal palace rise up before you,
circled by hundreds of screeching Ectovults. You
can fully grasp the size of the palace only when you
near its enormous entrance. The building is many
hundreds of yards high and is, formed, it seems,
from the same crystal you have been travelling on.
You enter a mighty chamber, and the chariot stops.
You climb out just as another robed figure rushes
up. 'You're late!' he hisses. 'Our Master returns and
his broth is not yet prepared! If you fail, you will
suffer his crystal breath. Hurry!' You follow him

across the chamber into another of similar size, in which a weird cauldron sits. Approaching, you realize that it is a goblet over three feet high, fashioned for some mighty hand. Another cowled figure sits stirring the brew within, waiting for you to empty your sack. You pour the contents into the cauldron and watch it darken to a murky green. The two cowled figures depart silently, leaving you alone with the goblet. If you drink some of the broth, turn to 45. If you add something to it, turn to 131. If you knock it over, turn to 365.

213

Pressing straight on, you find the undergrowth creeping on to the path ahead of you. Soon it becomes difficult to push your way through it. You laboriously hack your way through (lose 1 point of STAMINA), finally reaching a clearing from which three other paths lead. If you take the path on the left, turn to 123. If you take the centre path, turn to 132. If you take the path on the right, turn to 32.

214

There are three dark shapes. As they creep into the firelight you see that they are Black Elves. Two of them begin to go through your baggage, while the third approaches you warily. Choosing your moment with care, you wait until the Elf is bending over you before acting. Your sword sweeps in a wide arc, coming to a juddering halt in his side. He crumples and you leap to your feet, jerking your sword from the lifeless body. The other two Elves turn with a yelp, dropping your possessions. Turn to **120**.

215

The roaring gets louder, and you can see nothing in the blackness ahead. Then you are dashed against something hard and metallic. The river plunges down through a grating, but you are safe. Casting around, you find that the grating is littered with objects. You grab a few, then feel your way across the grating, showered by spray as you go. The grating leads to a tunnel set in the rock, a tunnel dimly lit by luminescent algae. Down the slimy tunnel are creeping two reptilian Kokomokoa, squat green creatures with abnormally large heads and malicious yellow eyes. They drop the baskets they were carrying and attack.

	SKILL	STAMINA
First KOKOMOKOA	5	6
Second KOKOMOKOA	5	5

If you do not have your sword, you fight at −2, and may not strike *killing blows*. If you defeat them, turn to **187**.

216

Many years ago, Barolo was your tutor in the treacherous north lands. He gave you your fine sword when he felt that you had learned enough from him to deserve it. He welcomes you warmly to his house and apologizes for its dilapidated condition. While you sit recounting some of your past adventures, he takes your sword and cradles it lovingly in his hand, testing its weight and balance. Your story is interrupted by a faint scrabbling from the corner of the room. You are about to get up to investigate, but Barolo acts faster. Before you can turn your head, he twists in his chair and the sword flies from his hands. You go to retrieve it and find it has impaled the still-twitching body of a rat. Barolo chuckles. 'The one technique I never taught you,' he says. 'It is not wise for a master to teach his pupil everything until he knows he can truly trust him or her.' Barola tells you that he is now prepared to hand his last secret on to you if you wish, but you will need to sacrifice the rest of the night's sleep to learn it. If you wish to learn how to throw your sword, turn to **226**. If you would rather get some rest, turn to **375**.

217

A spark leaps from your tinder and lodges in the dry cloth. You cup your hand round it and blow frantically. The spark takes, and the Jheera starts to smoulder. Looking up, you see the pulsing blackness nearly upon you. Turn to **199**.

218

You lower yourself slowly down the wall until you are level with the window. Then you crane your head round to peer through it. Inside, Dunyazad of Ikhtiyan sits on the floor, carefully packing clothing and jewellery into a small iron-bound trunk. Obviously she is preparing for an urgent journey . . . or escape. You heave yourself back up on to the roof. If this was the third window you looked in, turn to **25**. Otherwise, you may return to your quarters (turn to **151**), or investigate any of the following if you have not done so already:

The far left wall	Turn to **397**
The left centre wall	Turn to **94**
The far right wall	Turn to **340**

219

You pass through a band of cloud into the starry void you fell through earlier. Above you, a wall of cells hangs impossibly. The moans of the prisoners spur you on but, when you reach the top of the chain, you realize just how hopeless their plight is. There are no doors into their cells, only thick iron bars. You have found the stolen spirits of Kallamehr's countryfolk, victims of Bythos's hornets. Their earthly bodies exist only as zombie-like shells. Frustrated, you climb back down the chain and set out in search of a means of freeing them. If you follow the creaking sound, turn to **237**. Otherwise, turn to **203**.

220

You pretend to surrender, then make a running jump at the weakest-looking priest. As you near him you launch yourself into the air. Unfortunately he raises his staff, catching you a stinging blow on your side. Deduct 2 points of STAMINA. You crash to the ground and are quickly subdued. The priests begin to search you. If you have the Golden Fist, turn to **73**. If you do not have the Golden Fist, turn to **379**.

221

The way ahead begins to slope downwards, and the forest floor beneath your feet starts to soften. Soon you are squelching through boggy ground, with mud sucking at your shins. Flies begin to home in on you, and the heat saps your strength. Lose 1

point of STAMINA. After an hour's painful progress, the ground begins to rise and the track you
are on turns sharply to the left. There is nothing to
distinguish this part of the forest from any of the
others you have been through, so you push on.
Tick off a time box and turn to **366**.

222

The corpse tumbles backwards into the wine, which
laps over it. You pause a moment, but there is no
motion. If you examine the body, turn to **142**.
If you wish to leave the cellar straight away, turn
to **297**.

223

You gallop back the way you came, pausing from
time to time to refill your water-bottle. As you spur
your mare over a grassy rise, you suddenly find
yourself struggling with the reins when she rears
up. Something has disturbed her, something which
lies ahead. You can see nothing, but you catch the
faintest trace of a sour, musty smell. After some
coaxing, your horse continues reluctantly down
into the valley and along the narrow track which
winds its way up the hillside opposite. You have to
pick your way carefully up the steep path, but
finally you top the ridge and look down into the
valley. Off to your left you can see a column of
smoke rising. Check the time boxes on your *Adventure Sheet*. If you have already marked ten or more
time boxes, turn to **251**. Otherwise, tick off a time
box and turn to **95**.

As he approaches the keep, Ramedes lets out a blood-curdling roar. He flings the door open and smashes a guard aside with the flaming brand. Then he is inside the keep. You run across the courtyard as screams and yells begin to fill the air. When you reach the gate, you are nearly floored by the body of a guard which comes tumbling out. Inside, in a small entry-hall, Ramedes is battling six guards, though more lie bloodied and motionless around the chamber. He is swinging a halberd as if it were a sickle, but these guards are wiser, waiting for the hero to tire before they strike. One is winding a crossbow and, as you enter the hall, sword at the ready, he lets fly the bolt. Ramedes takes it full in the chest and staggers backwards. He crashes to the ground and looks up at you accusingly. He has no time to speak, for the guards are upon him with their swords. Then they turn on you. Your adventure ends here.

225

Bythos strides impatiently towards the goblet. 'You were nearly late, Gatherer. You know the penalty for failure!' he says. If you have been told the 'secret of Bythos's power', turn to **374**. Otherwise, if you have eaten the herbs from Sige's pomander, turn to **31**. If you wish to flee, turn to **335**. You may hold up the Golden Fist, if you have it (turn to **389**). Or you may attack him with your sword (turn to **161**).

226

The technique that Barolo calls the Spitting Fly is to be used against an opponent only in direst need. By using it, you disarm yourself, so you must be certain that your blow will be a fatal one. It may not be used in the midst of battle, for you must relax your body completely. You spend the rest of the night practising and, although you can never hope to match the speed and accuracy of Barolo, you become quite adept at hitting the targets Barolo sets up for you. Next morning you greet the dawn bleary-eyed and stiff of limb. Turn to **19**.

227

You loose your bolt at the jeering jailer, praying that it will pass between the bars of the grille. Sure enough, it finds its mark, impaling the evil man in mid-cackle. He slumps on to the grille, the trapdoor keys dangling from his twitching hands. You scramble up the rough walls of the pit, observing as you do that Ramedes has swung over to below the jailer's body, reached through the grille and grasped the keys. Soon you are both out of the pit, recovering from your ordeal. Turn to **10**.

228

You are standing amid the glowing golden powder when a tall, cowled figure steps over the rim of the bowl. He stops his chanting when he sees you and stoops to pick up a small shard of crystal with a skeletal hand. He takes each end and pulls it out until he holds a ragged crystal javelin, which he then hurls at you. Instinctively, you raise your sword to parry. Roll two dice. If the result is *less than* your SKILL, turn to **360**. If it is *greater than or equal to* your SKILL, turn to **274**.

229

You are no threat to the legendary acrobats of Granat. Your grab for the opening falls pitifully short, and you plunge headlong to the ground, landing painfully on your shoulder. Lose 1 point of STAMINA. As you lie panting, you notice the hut is descending towards you. The spindly legs are bending! Soon you are through the opening. Turn to **372**.

230

You hurry down the tunnel, back towards the river, constantly looking over your shoulder. Then you stumble over something. Looking down, you see a tentacle. Turn to **343**.

231

As you push onward, you notice clusters of foul-smelling fungus growing on either side of the path. You have to pick your way carefully along the path to avoid disturbing them – in case they carry poisonous spores. You begin to remember tales told of southern forests in which you can lose yourself in a maze of shifting trackways, wandering in circles until death from hunger and exhaustion catches up with you. Ahead of you, the trail divides into two. You may take the trail which slopes downwards slightly and to the left (turn to **213**), or try the other, which leads off to the right (turn to **32**).

232

You twist to the left, avoiding the blow, but roll into your fire. Although it was beginning to die out, you are still badly burned. Lose 2 points of STAMINA. You beat the burning embers off your singed tunic and face your opponent, weaponless. He is a Black Elf, and behind him are two more of his kin. As you have no weapon, you must fight at −2 to your SKILL, and you cannot score *killing blows*.

First BLACK ELF   SKILL 7   STAMINA 6

If you win, you may retrieve your sword before the other two Elves are upon you. Turn to **120**.

233

You dive into the river but, weighed down as you are by your equipment, it is all you can do to resist the strong current which threatens to sweep you down-river. Soon the Troll spots you and begins to throw rocks at you. Struggling helplessly amid the wild water, you are a sitting target. A large rock strikes you on the head and you are carried away by the current. Your sword is swept from your scabbard and is lost to the wild water as you sink into unconsciousness. Lose 1 point of STAMINA. Tick off a time box and turn to **89**.

234

As you make your way down to the courtyard you hear a blood-curdling scream. Diving through the door near by, you find yourself in the kitchen. A figure, wreathed in flames, staggers about the room as various servants vainly fling water at it. After a few seconds the fiery figure collapses. The cook turns to you. 'It's Janas the page. He just ran in here clutching his chest and flung himself on the fire,' she says. The boy is dead. Though shocked and mystified by the tragedy, you prepare to leave. You can do nothing here. Turn to **140**.

235

You dismount and face the multitude of blank-eyed peasants as bravely as you can. Several of them set down the palanquin they bear, and from it steps a richly dressed man, his face deeply scored, his eyes burning with malevolence. His silent horde makes no move towards you, but the man gestures them to advance, his movements calm and deliberate. He speaks: 'You'll pay for the slaughter of my winged servants. You'll pay with your life.' Before you stands the unsmiling general of this warped army. Kallamehr's fate lies in your hands. If you have the Reaver's bottle and wish to show it, turn to **55**. Otherwise, if you know the Spitting Fly and wish to use it, turn to **260**. Or you may attack him (turn to **65**).

236

The rope slips rapidly out through the smoke-hole in the ceiling, just as the first villager bursts into the hut. They seem relieved to find you still alive. As the buzzing sound fades away, you race out of the hut. Silhouetted against the moon is a huge marrow-shaped object which hangs impossibly in the starry sky. You watch as it dwindles into the distance. Then you turn to the villagers you have elected to protect. They huddle pathetically around you. You have abandoned your true mission in favour of this lowly settlement. Kallamehr is doomed. Your adventure ends here.

237

Cautiously you advance, observing more of the darting shadows beneath the crystal floor. The creaking gets louder, and suddenly a crack appears almost beneath your feet. Then the crystal shatters and a black shape erupts through it, spraying you with oily black water. The black shape shoots up into the clouds, and you scrabble for a footing on the shifting crystal. Roll two dice. If the result is *less than* your SKILL, turn to 339. If the result is *greater than or equal to* your SKILL, turn to 93.

238

You turn dejectedly back to your horse, but stagger as you feel something coiling round your leg. It is a large snake; angrily, you raise your sword to cut it down. Before you can strike, the snake speaks softly. 'Don't you recognize me? I am Caduceus.

Bythos has fled to the Abyss. You must follow him there if you wish to save these people, for Enthymesis has failed. The river in this valley flows underground and passes through a cavern in which there is a gateway to that region. Go now, lose no time.' He slithers away and you hurry over to the river. Using a rotting log as a makeshift raft, you are soon racing with the current. Turn to **89**.

239
You wake up in a dank cell. Your whole body aches from the beating the priests have given you (lose 2 points of STAMINA). You still have all your possessions with you, except the Golden Fist (cross it off your *Adventure Sheet*). After making you wait for several hours, a priest arrives at your cell. He tells you reluctantly that you are to be freed, on the orders of Lady Dunyazad. Soon you have your horse back, and you are off once more. Tick off two time boxes and turn to **7**.

240
Your bolt rebounds from the metal grille and, before you can reload, the jailer has backed away from the grille, abandoning you to your fate. Turn to **352**.

241

You smash the javelin aside. The Gatherer reaches down for another piece of crystal, but you are too quick for him. You leap at him as he lifts his crystal weapon.

GATHERER	SKILL 6	STAMINA 6

If you defeat him, turn to **318**.

242

You must fight the guards.

	SKILL	STAMINA
First GUARD	7	8
Second GUARD	6	7

You have to fight both the guards together. At the beginning of each Attack Round, you must decide which of the two you are going to fight; resolve the battle against him as normal. You should also roll two dice to determine your Attack Strength against the other guard, then two dice again for his Attack Strength against you for that Attack Round. You will not injure him if your Attack Strength is greater, you will simply parry his blow. If his Attack Strength is greater than yours, then he will wound you in the normal way. If you defeat both the guardsmen, turn to **150**.

243

Many hours go by while you scour the forest for snake food. Tick off a time box, then return to **395** and try again. If you run out of time or LUCK, your adventure is over.

244

As you approach the row of puppets, your left foot squelches in something and skids. You have trodden in a sticky green footprint, one of a line which leads from the cupboard to the table and back again. The cupboard before you is crudely daubed with a rune: the sign of a single arrow. If you open the cupboard with your sword, ready to strike, turn to **76**. If you open it normally, turn to **37**.

245

A tall cowled figure walks into the bowl, chanting all the time, and reverently collects up the golden powder into a silken sack. He is chanting 'Broth for my Master! Broth for Bythos! Magical broth makes the Master of the Abyss!' If you spring to attack him, turn to **154**. If you creep round the rim of the bowl to surprise him as he leaves, turn to **40**. If you follow him as he leaves, turn to **112**.

246

Your manoeuvre is successful. You grip his weapon hand firmly and drive your free hand into his jaw, throwing him off balance. With a neat flick of the wrist, you force the knife from his grip, and send him tumbling to the floor. As he does so, you recognize the grizzled features of your old blade-master, Barolo. He has changed greatly in the past years, and now sports a wooden leg; but he looks pleased to see you. 'Good as ever, eh, young 'un? Lucky I was going easy on you or I'd have had you on a dinner plate by now.' Turn to **216**.

247

With a mighty kick of your legs you push yourself down. Your lungs are bursting as your hand alights on the hilt of the fabulous sword, and blood pounds in your head. The effort of freeing the sword proves too much and your breath escapes in an explosion of bubbles. Desperately you thrash your way upwards, only to be caught between two of the lower bars. As water enters your lungs you curse your greed.

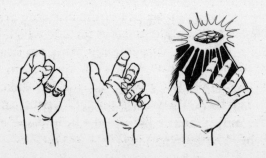

248

You evade the Troll, leaving him to try to digest his troublesome meal, and make your way back to the river. There you hurry along the path which leads along the bank. Turn to **133**.

249

You dismount and approach the bundle cautiously. As you draw closer, you realize that this is no bundle, but a body! You turn over the corpse, to reveal the familiar features of Sophia of Blacksand. You draw back your hand rapidly when it begins to sting painfully. A greyish slime seems to have eaten into Sophia's lower body and legs. She must have been the hero sent to scout out the invading army, but you cannot begin to guess at the fate which has overcome her. You contemplate your choices of action. If you continue with your mission to the northern army, turn to **301**. If you choose to take on Sophia's mission and scout to the east, tick off a time box and turn to **329**. If you return to Kallamehr to report, tick off a time box and turn to **394**.

250

You watch as the former prisoners each take a sip of the blue liquid. One by one they dissolve away in a blue glow, until you are left with only the Servants for company. You look down sadly at the empty bowl, wondering how long it will be before the Servants can fill it once more. You can only guess. The Servants explain that, as Ruler of the Abyss, you gain the power of all the lost magical items of Allansia which are drawn to this realm, but it is small consolation for your exile here. If you have the wound which changes colour, turn to **400**. If not, turn to **119**.

251

After a brisk ride you reach the village and pull up before the open gates. A line of villagers is silently marching out through them and off down the road. You hail them, but they do not even turn their heads. Mystified, you edge closer. A well-dressed figure detaches itself from the villagers and saunters towards you. The man is munching distractedly at a rib of pork. He tosses the bone over his shoulder, and turns his attention to you, fixing you with a penetrating gaze. 'Ah, it is you,' he says, apparently satisfied. With a casual wave of his arm he gestures at you. 'Take this wretch,' he says as he turns back to the village. Turn to **113**.

252

As you leave the courtyard, you remember that you have seen no sign of the other heroes who were left to defend the city, apart from Luthaur who was at the funeral. Where have they gone? Making discreet inquiries at the Parrot-in-a-Cage Inn, you discover that they all met with unfortunate accidents. One mysteriously vanished while walking the ramparts at night; another accidentally shot himself with a crossbow. Still another was found impaled on one of the swords carried by the Statue of Justice. There are many ways to meet an untimely end in Kallamehr. Yours is particularly bizarre. You are walking down an empty street when –

253

None of the Murkurons has seen you enter the room. You realize that three of them are holding the door shut, while the fourth is intoning a spell: a fiery glow is spreading from his fingers. Then he notices you and pauses, his face struck by panic. 'Ylech'nya Pipphen!' says a voice in your head. If you attack the Murkuron, turn to **173**. If you run to the door, turn to **48**.

254

As you step between the narrow legs, you notice an opening in the floor of the hut above you. You are just wondering how on earth you are going to make it up there when the hut begins to lower, the spindly legs bending. You position yourself directly under the opening as the hut descends towards you. Turn to **372**.

255

He is a sitting target. Convulsed with laughter, he can do nothing to dodge the blade which flies from your hands. It catches him in the belly, and he is still laughing as he starts to topple . . . turn to **302**.

256

The road is deeply rutted, as if it is often used, but you meet no other travellers. On the slopes around you the vegetation grows thicker, and soon you are riding through woodland. Then, ahead of you on the road, you see a charging ox. It thunders past, bellowing madly. A little further on, you see the cart that it had been shackled to, ditched by the roadside. Near by lies the still body of another ox; you sense movement behind it, and hear revolting sucking noises. You canter up cautiously. Suddenly your horse whinnies, and a black-swathed figure looks up. You cannot penetrate the darkness beneath its hood, but you feel a malevolent gaze trained upon you. With an inhuman shriek, the figure races off into the undergrowth with a loping gait. If you give chase, turn to **296**. If you examine the ox and cart, turn to **13**.

257

You race towards the Gatherer, but he hastily prepares another javelin. Turn to **105**.

258

The liquid tastes sour, but it is in fact a Luck Potion. You may restore your LUCK to its *Initial* level, and increase that *Initial* level by 1 point. Now turn back to the paragraph you just left.

259

You hurl your sword at the jeering jailer, praying that it will pass between the bars of the grille. Sure enough, it finds its mark, impaling the evil man in mid-cackle. He slumps on to the grille, the trapdoor keys dangling from his twitching hands. You scramble up the rough walls of the pit, observing as you do that Ramedes has swung over to below the jailer's body, reached through the grille and grasped the keys. Soon you are both out of the pit, recovering from your ordeal. Turn to **10**.

260

Your sword streaks towards your enemy, but he is too fast for you. His own sword flashes from its scabbard and deflects yours harmlessly into the ground. 'You are not the only one who knows that trick,' he says, hurling his blade at you. You have no time to dodge; his sword impales you through the chest.

261

You approach the well, but your way is barred by several burly peasants, shouting: 'You're not welcome here, horse-thief!' They don't look the sort to listen to reason, so you spur your horse out of the village. Turn to **7**.

262

You grab your possessions and clamber out of the window. Just as you are lowering yourself down, the door collapses and a blast of flame guts the bedroom. It is not a great drop to the ground, and you land clumsily but unscathed. Turn to **111**.

263

As you step into the sand you feel a tugging at your feet. You wade further into it, and sink up to your knees. A few seconds later, you cannot move your legs, and the sand is up to your waist. As your head sinks lower you take a deep breath, hoping it is not going to be your last. Turn to **383**.

264

You unfold the scrap of paper. On it is written: 'Beware – you are watched by a thousand eyes.' You ponder what this strange message can mean, but are brought out of your reverie when you realize that you are being addressed by Dunyazad of Ikhtiyan. She seems insulted that you have failed to hear her question, and scowls at you. At the same time, the hairs on the nape of your neck prickle. You feel certain that someone in the room is watching you carefully – a little too carefully. The meal over, you prepare to depart. Turn to **234**.

265

Ants are still crawling over your body, biting you viciously. Lose 1 point of STAMINA. You roll around in the dirt and beat them off desperately. You tear off your clothes and brush yourself with leaves, then beat your clothes against a tree to rid them of the pests. Turn to **58**.

266

Bythos curses as you grab the chain, and launches a punch. He catches you in the stomach, and you gasp in pain as a chill blast is forced out of you. If you now let go of the chain and attack Bythos, turn to **196**. If you blow on him, turn to **380**.

267

As darkness falls, you lie awake on your pallet, trying to make some sense of the day's events. As you ponder, you feel the hairs on the back of your neck rise. Straining your senses, you make out a faint, familiar buzzing. Your enemy is within the palace! You snatch up your sword and rush into the courtyard. Looking across at the keep, you see a black shadow rise from it and disappear into the night sky. The keep is the dwelling-place of Kallamehr's nobility: its central tower contains Lady Carolina's private suite and audience-chamber. The winged creature flew not from the tower itself but from one of the windows of the keep from which the tower springs. Tick off a time box. If you go and investigate the keep, turn to **342**. If you return to your pallet, turn to **165**.

268

A little way down the path you enter a small glade. In the centre you can see a slightly raised mound of loose earth with a neat circular opening just above ground level. From it protrudes a black human hand, scrabbling in the loose soil as if trying to get a grip. As you approach, you realize that the hand's colour is caused by a crawling layer of ants. If you rush to the man's aid and try to save him, turn to **300**. If you would rather not take the risk, turn to **211**.

269

The Troll glances round as you approach, and you see him look down at a crossbow bolt protruding from his shoulder, then stare at the crossbow you have slung from your belt. Trolls may be stupid, but they never forget someone who has hurt them. He leaps to his feet and charges at you, brandishing the sapling like a club.

TROLL   SKILL 9   STAMINA 7

If you defeat the Troll, turn to **207**.

270

If you have a blow-pipe, turn to **2**. Otherwise, if you have not yet examined the puppets and cupboard closely, you may do so (turn to **244**). Alternatively, you may leave the building and make your way out of the settlement (turn to **22**).

271

You quickly nock a bolt and let it fly. It curves in a lazy arc, seeming to lose all its power. It floats gently to the ground, far short of its target. Turn to 322.

272

You lie flat and hold your breath as the footsteps of the guard come closer. Then they pause. A voice rings out: 'All right, you. On your feet. Now.' Reluctantly you clamber to your feet and turn to face the guardsman who is covering you with a crossbow. He calls out, and soon you are circled by guards who escort you along the walkway to the guardhouse, where you are warned to stay in your quarters. A guardsman is given instructions to make sure you don't try any more midnight wandering. Turn to 165.

273

The trail ploughs straight through the trees, and you traipse along it for an hour or so, with nothing relieving the monotony. Tick off a time box and turn to 366.

274

You time your sword-sweep badly, and the javelin thuds into your shoulder. Grabbing its shaft, you watch in terror as your body starts to crystallize. Your adventure ends here.

275

If you have drunk Bythos's broth, turn to 280. If you have the Golden Fist and wish to hold it up, turn to 141. If you would rather attack Bythos with your sword, turn to 78.

276

Next morning, you peer out at the servants scurrying about the courtyard. They erect a kind of low stage, with a platform behind it. Soon a coffin is brought out and laid with great care on the low stage by a number of priests. You guess that the coffin is Lady Carolina's, and that her body is being brought out so that her subjects may pay their last respects. Madhaerios, Dunyazad of Ikhtiyan, Asiah Albudur and Sige the Silent all file out and take their places on the platform overlooking the catafalque. Then the guards open the gates and allow the citizens to file reverently in. When the courtyard is full of people, you leave your hiding-place and mingle with them. Turn to 344.

277

You wade into the river and are quickly caught by the current. When you reach the iron bars, you find them sturdy and unmovable. Feeling down with your feet, you find that they extend a good distance beneath the surface of the river. If you swim back to the bank and investigate the tunnel, turn to 24. If you try to swim under the grille, turn to 127.

278

You continue to toss and turn uncomfortably. Deduct 2 points of STAMINA and tick off a time box. While staring at the skylight in the ceiling you suddenly become aware of a rich, acrid smell. You wrinkle your nose, trying to trace its source, then realize that the room is filling up with swirling smoke. The door is outlined with a red glow, and you can feel the heat coming from it. A loud buzzing noise from the window distracts you; looking over to it, you see a black-cloaked figure which hovers just *outside*. If you rush straight over to attack the figure with your fists, turn to **188**. If you go to grab your sword, turn to **361**.

279

With consummate grace, Sige rises to her feet and looks around her. She walks slowly over to the coffin and stands before it. She lowers her head towards Carolina, then stops and straightens up again. She speaks, and though her voice sounds as quiet as the breath of a breeze upon grass, you know that it can be heard in every part of the courtyard. 'Why must I bow before the orders of this lying upstart? This is intolerable, an obscenity!' She is trembling with rage, but her features remain as placid as ever.

Then a brave soul from the crowd shouts out, 'Pay your respects!' and the crowd back him up with shouts and calls. '*Quiet!*' Sige silences the crowd with one word. Then she bends over Carolina once more. An instant later, she has grasped the jewelled Sword of Office from the dead fingers which held it, and swings it violently at you. You twist to deflect the blow, but the flat of the blade catches you painfully on the shoulder. Lose 2 points of STAMINA. Now you must battle Sige, the traitor of Kallamehr.

SIGE THE SILENT   SKILL 7   STAMINA 5

If you defeat her, turn to 384.

280

The nauseous feeling you had when you drank Bythos's brew returns even more strongly. You gag involuntarily, then whine in pain as your body twists and buckles. Your robe is split as you burst out of it, growing all the time. Bythos stands aghast, watching your transformation. 'No! Not you! There can be only one Master!' he howls. He draws in his breath sharply, then lets out a freezing blast at you. The crystals which form on your skin quickly melt and drip from you, and you advance on him. He dodges to one side, then leaps for the wall. With a blow from his fist, he smashes a jagged hole in it and leaps through. If you leap through the hole after him, turn to 299. If you leave the chamber through the door you came in by, turn to 354.

281

The buzzing sound soon fades away, but you are glad you chose to be careful. Pushing through a wall of undergrowth you find yourself staring down into a deep gorge. You search all round the edge of the precipice, and scan the bottom of the gorge for signs of your quarry, but you see nothing. Somehow he has vanished into thin air. Turn to **139**.

282

Aletheia is despondent, but you remember the Troll you saw carrying a sapling by the banks of the river. Quickly, you describe the tree to her, and she confirms that it is indeed the Jheera. 'You must go at once and rescue the leaves,' she says. 'I control the paths of the shifting forest – follow the trail and you will reach the river. When you have the leaves, the path will lead you safely back to the glade where you left your horse. Be sure you never return to this place – I will not be so welcoming a second time!' You hurry from the hut and along the only path leading out of the clearing. Minutes later, you reach the river at the spot where you saw the Troll. You find his clumsy footprints in the soft mud and follow them into the forest. A little way in, you come upon him crouching by a large hole in the ground, vainly trying to poke the sapling into it. If you shot a crossbow bolt at the Troll when you saw him earlier, turn to **269**. If not, turn to **122**.

283

Mema grips your mare's mane firmly with both hands. She lets out a whimper of terror, then points into the black army. At first you cannot see what she is pointing at, then you notice a pulsing black mist hanging in the air. If you have washed the green slime off Mema, turn to **16**. If not, turn to **69**.

284

A spark leaps from your tinder and lodges in the dry cloth. You cup your hand round it and blow frantically, but succeed only in extinguishing it. In your haste you have dropped your tinder-box, and you look up to see the cloud of black hornets almost upon you. Turn to **113**.

285

The brownish liquid tastes sweet and not at all unpleasant. Your stomach warms to it, and after a short while you notice a tingling sensation in your feet. However, nothing else seems to happen, and soon even the tingling fades away. Turn back to the paragraph you just left.

286

A single blow is enough to unbalance the statue. It totters, then tips over and shatters. Sige picks herself up from the ruined crystal and bows. 'You have my eternal gratitude,' she says, 'and in return I must give you something: the secret of Bythos's power. On this plane, magical items and charms are useless, but Fangthane steel bites true. Bythos has no defence against such a blade, so don't let him trick you. I bid you farewell.' She hurries off into the mist; you make to follow, but soon lose sight of her. As you continue, you hear an ominous creaking sound. Turn to **237**.

287

You find the going is hard across country, and you waste precious time trying to find the best way round a wood before getting back on to a road. Tick off two time boxes and turn to **7**.

288

The mighty walls that seemed so secure when you passed through the city gates somehow look less sturdy from the inside. A frightened city is huddled behind them, and looking out of the window you sense the people's fear. You turn and find yourself gazing at your reflection in the ornate mirror opposite. What have you let yourself in for? You may be a hero, but that doesn't mean you don't get scared. You focus on your image in the mirror, catching a fuzzy reflection of the darkening window. Suddenly you are in darkness, save for a dim reddish glow. There is a scrabbling at the window, but you are unable to tear your eyes from the mirror. A hideously scarred and discoloured figure drags himself through the opening. More twisted fingers and hands claw the sill behind him as he lurches towards you. You scream, and jerk your body round to face the horror (turn to **174**).

289

The jailer lies dead at your feet, but you know that you are too late to save his captive from a horrible fate. You will have to find somewhere to spend the rest of the night in safety. If you wish to hide in the stables, turn to **137**. If you go back to your pallet in the servants' quarters, turn to **165**.

290

You pass through rich cultivated lands, the estates of the wealthy nobles of Kallamehr, until you see the welcoming sight of the Rangor Tower up ahead. Tick off a time box and turn to **67**.

291

As he topples to the ground, Bythos sneers: 'You may have defeated me, but the people of Kallamehr will float in the void for ever!' You return to the palace, where the Servants proclaim you the new Ruler of the Abyss, but your victory is an empty one. You have failed Kallamehr.

292

You drop on your knees and spin round, reaching to grab his weapon arm with your left hand, and pushing with your right. Roll two dice. If the result is *less than* your SKILL, turn to **246**. If the result is *greater than or equal to* your SKILL, turn to **178**.

293

In the leather pouch is a large round locket, intricately crafted from platinum and other rare metals. It is set with blue stones, arranged in what is unmistakably the Seal of the House of Rangor. The clasp is carved in the shape of two interlocked silver dolphins; try as you may, you cannot prise them apart, though you feel that it is only magical power which is keeping them together. Stowing the locket away carefully, you settle down for the night. The commotion in the courtyard has subsided. Tick off a time box. Turn to **276**.

294

You pull yourself up and on to the metal ring, then begin your slow progress up the smooth metallic chain. Roll one die. If you roll 1–4, turn to **124**. If you roll 5 or 6, turn to **219**.

'That heady mash of herbs you carry does more than you may think,' says the woman. 'You will know of its sleep-stealing properties, I warrant. But its powers on this plane are as nothing compared to those it holds in the Abyss. Eaten in that mystic region it will protect you from the Master's crystal breath. Eaten here, it will turn your stomach – that is all! You are very lucky to have such a gift; the Paa, Maet and Teth herbs are extremely rare.' As she speaks, you feel a soft weight upon your shoulders. You turn your head to find yourself staring into the eyes of a serpent. You shudder and automatically grab for it. But it is too fast for you. In an instant its thick coils are wrapped around your neck. 'Meet Caduceus,' says the woman. Make a note of the names of the herbs in order on your *Adventure Sheet* and turn to **307**.

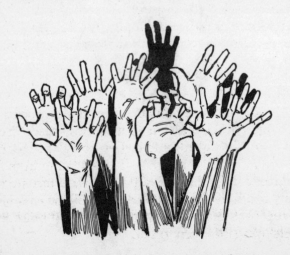

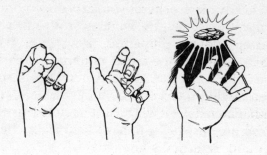

296

Dismounting with a single bound, you crash off into the greenery after the black-clad fiend. After a few minutes you are forced to stop for a second to clamber over a fallen log. As you do so, you hear the crack of breaking undergrowth, followed by a loud buzzing sound coming from ahead of you. If you sprint towards the noise, hoping to catch up with its source, turn to **373**. If you move forward cautiously, turn to **281**.

297

You wade frantically towards the steps, gripped by an irrational compulsion to leave this place. Your fear is proved well founded when you glance back to see the man you thought you killed rising from the wine and staggering towards you. You race up the steps and slam the trapdoor, then roll the cask back on top of it. As you leave the shop the pounding starts up again. Turn to **128**.

298

You bow your head and raise your hands in mock surrender. Then, in one fluid motion, you reach back with your right hand to grasp the hilt of your sword from its scabbard on your back. Before the guard can even register surprise and loose off a bolt from his crossbow, the sword flies from its scabbard and straight into his midriff. He topples back soundlessly on to the walkway. You hurry up and retrieve the sword. You may also take the guard's crossbow if you wish, though it is rather cumbersome. Then you push his body off the wall, down into the courtyard. Turn to **71**.

299

You are right behind Bythos as he flees across the crystal wastes. He finally slides to a halt at a place where a chain leads up into the clouds from a hoop in the ground. He grabs it and starts to tug, but before he can break the chain you are upon him.

BYTHOS   SKILL 10   STAMINA 10

You may not use your sword, so you may not strike *killing blows*. If you have it, you may not use Barolo's buckler either, so you lose the SKILL bonus it normally gives you. If you defeat Bythos, turn to **108**.

300

As you grasp the poor fellow's hand and start to pull, the ants begin crawling from his hand on to yours. By the time you have him pulled free of the ant-hill, your arm is a mass of biting ants. But they are driven from your mind by the sight of the man you have rescued: he is covered from head to foot with ants, and seems none the worse for it. He is a Symbiote, a foul mutant who lives with the ants that cover him in mutual co-operation. The ants which are biting your arms are beginning to draw blood (lose 1 point of STAMINA), and you realize that they are softening you up so that their host can overcome you. You must kill him before you are eaten alive!

ANT SYMBIOTE	SKILL 6	STAMINA 10

Every time the Symbiote wins an Attack Round against you, more ants will crawl on to you and begin biting. Make a note of how many Attack Rounds the Symbiote wins. When he has won three, there will be so many ants on you that you will lose an additional 1 point of STAMINA per round. If you defeat the Symbiote, turn to **265**.

301

The remainder of your journey passes uneventfully. You arrive on the borders of Kallamehr and deliver your sealed scroll to Commander Yunan. He seems unwilling to divide his forces, but must obey the Lady Carolina's commands. Soon you are riding south once more, this time at the head of a column of soldiers. Several days later, you breast a hill and see the city of Kallamehr below. With the army behind you, you ride down towards it. Turn to **182**.

302

The Slave Master crashes to the ground, his body shattering as if made of china. From the shards emerges a wisp of black smoke, which grows and twists . . . into the shape of the man you just slew. He smiles confidently and drifts towards you. His arms encircle you and lift you off the ground. His blurred, smoky features are close to your face, and only his eyes retain their sharpness. 'I am Bythos, Master of the Abyss,' he says defiantly. 'Though you have destroyed my earthly shell, yet I live on.

Kallamehr is still mine, taken from within. You will not rob me of victory! I have the spirits of these people in thrall. They will remain trapped in the Abyss for eternity!' His smoky form dissipates and you fall to the ground. Around you stand the people of Kallamehr, empty and unmoving. You can do nothing for them. Turn to **238**.

You fire once more at the beast. Again you are rewarded by a cry of pain from below, but at the same time the dangling man lets out a despairing gasp as he loses his grip and plummets downwards. There is a sickening sucking noise, followed by a muffled shriek, and then the gurgling begins once more. You have no time to contemplate the poor man's fate, however. The light in the room flickers, and you whirl round to see a spindly figure racing out of the chamber, a flaming torch in his hand. You pursue him. The twisted jailer flees up the stairs, but you catch him at the top. He turns to fight, swinging the torch wildly.

JAILER   SKILL 5   STAMINA 5

Every time the jailer wins an Attack Round, roll one die. If the result is 1–3, you simply lose the usual 2 points of STAMINA. If the result is 4–6, however, then your clothing catches alight. Because of this, you will lose 1 additional point of STAMINA during each following Attack Round (whether the jailer hits you or not), until you kill the jailer and can put out the flames. If you defeat the jailer, turn to **289**.

304

You brave the smoke to grab your possessions, toss them out of the window, and then follow yourself, edging over the sill until you are dangling by your fingertips and looking down in readiness for the fall. Suddenly you sense a presence above you. If you look up, turn to **148**. If you let go immediately, turn to **97**.

305

You launch a flying kick at the Crystal Warrior, hoping to unbalance it. Sure enough, it wobbles unsteadily, and you seize the chance to grab its hammer. Roll two dice. If the result is *less than* your SKILL, turn to **62**. If it is *greater than or equal to* your SKILL, turn to **398**.

306

There are thousands upon thousands of people in the army you face, yet no sound comes from them save the tramp of boots in the dirt. You are now close enough to observe the advancing front rank. You expected to see barbarians from Kulak Isle, mercenaries, Orcs, or other dire creatures of Evil. The truth is far more shocking. Peasants – men, women and children – march listlessly towards you. They carry no weapons, but you have no doubt of their destructive powers. Turn to 113.

307

'The best companion of all is he. Loyal, yet independent!' she says. You smile uncomfortably, praying that Caduceus will soon find something else to wrap himself around. Aletheia continues: 'The plague which is upon this land is spread not by rats.' She raises her arms above her head once more and conjures another vision. It is a swirling cloud of huge black hornets. The vision disappears, and she speaks again. 'These parasites can steal a man's spirit with their stings, banishing it to the Abyss and leaving his body a slave to evil. And what warrior can fight off foes so tiny?' She pauses, as if deep in thought, then begins to create another vision. 'There is one way they can be defeated. The untainted leaf of the Jheera tree may be burnt to produce a fragrant smoke that is fatal to these soul-stealers. A young Jheera grows in the forest.' But as the vision forms, her face drops and she lets out a gasp of surprise. A pile of loose soil marks the spot where a tree has been uprooted . . . Turn to 282.

308

As you ride off he calls after you: 'I curse you, scoundrel! I will catch up with you one day and take my revenge!' You ride for another hour, certain that you've left Tasbadh far behind, then settle down for the rest of the night. Next morning, you are up bright and early, and continue your journey. Soon you enter a small village, in which you hope to refill your water bottle from the communal well. Tick off a time box. If you have the Golden Fist, turn to **121**. If not, turn to **261**.

309

Suddenly you hear a croak. You look about you and see a human face, embedded in a greenish slime. 'Beware!' it says. 'Maijem-Nosoth will return. I, Enthymesis, have failed in my task, and will pay with my life; but you may yet live. Take the whistle that lies at your feet; it will aid you in your fight. Stay away from the sands – they lead to the Realm of Bythos! Now beware – the beast returns!' You pick up a small silver whistle from the floor. If you flee down the passage you came along, turn to **230**. If you wait to face the horror, turn to **115**.

After several minutes, the slight form of Dunyazad breezes into the chamber, accompanied by a hulking bodyguard and a shifty, travel-stained individual whom you recognize as Luthaur, one of the other heroes who stayed behind to protect Kallamehr. 'What is it you want?' she snaps abruptly at you. You explain to her what you have discovered during your journey, and noticing as you do so a smirk appear on the face of the hero. When you finish, Dunyazad turns to him. 'Is this true?' she asks. 'No, my Lady,' he replies. 'As you know, I myself have just returned from scouting those very lands, and I saw no invading horde. It was just a wild story spread by some irresponsible rumour-monger – the superstitious villagers had merely abandoned their villages and hidden in the forests. Does this wastrel think to impress you with these ridiculous claims?' Dunyazad turns back to you and frowns. 'I am too busy with the arrangements for Lady Carolina's funeral to listen to you two bicker. I will use my own methods to ascertain the truth. Meanwhile you will spend the night in the palace.' You are led off to the servants' quarters and given a hard pallet to sleep on. Turn to **267**.

311

You search the bodies of the Elves, discovering 17 Gold Pieces and a golden statuette in the shape of a fist. The fingers are clenched around something that rattles as you pick up the golden trophy. Try as you might, you cannot unclench the fingers to reveal what lies within. Turn to **163**.

312

You forge ahead further into the heart of the forest. The trees begin to close in on you, crowding out the sunlight. The forest floor is now carpeted with bright green moss, and you find yourself making moderate progress on this springy turf. The atmosphere is close and humid, and you start to wheeze with the effort. Walking in this weather is exhausting. Lose 1 point of STAMINA as the hours of trudging pass. Finally you come upon a fork. If you take the right-hand path, turn to **231**. If you take the left-hand path, turn to **213**.

313

You pull off your cowl and face him defiantly. He leans down towards you and laughs. 'So you are Allansia's finest?' he says, and laughs again. Your adventure ends here.

314

The Quagrant fights by sucking its victims into its mouth and then stripping their flesh off.

QUAGRANT   SKILL 8   STAMINA 14

If you lose an attack to the Quagrant, it sucks you into its mouth. From then on, you will lose 2 points of STAMINA per Attack Round as it begins to suck the flesh off your bones *even if* you win the attack against it. If you defeat the Quagrant, turn to **64**.

She tells you her name is Mema, and that she is the apprentice of the enchanter Enthymesis. She knows little more than you of the reason why the village is deserted. She has stayed hidden in the cupboard for the last couple of days, since her master left. Before going, he told her to remain hidden, and he coated her in the green paste, which he said would protect her. She tells you that, the evening before his departure, Enthymesis had been very worried by a divination he had performed. He had told her that he had to undertake a dangerous journey to seek guidance from Aletheia the Sage who dwells in a shifting forest in the mountains to the north. Then he had insisted that she should stay hidden. Sure enough, she had remained cowering in the cupboard while a terrible din came down upon the settlement. Terrified, she listened to the hideous shrieks of the townsfolk. 'Finally silence descended on the village, then you came.' If you have not already searched the wizard's desk, you may do so now (turn to **333**). If you have already searched the desk, or if you don't wish to, you may leave the house with Mema (turn to **2**).

316
The creature collapses in a heap and twitches. Slowly it dissolves into a greenish sticky mess which steams and hisses. You step back from its revolting remains, into the sand. Turn to **263**.

317
You sleep well and awake refreshed in the morning. You recover 2 points of STAMINA. Turn to **19**.

318
As the Gatherer collapses, his robes fall open, revealing his shrivelled body. He has no possessions apart from a silken sack, so you peer over the rim of the bowl to find out where he has come from. You see a crystal chariot with two Ectovults tethered to it and a Crystal Sprite standing patiently near by. Turn to **27**.

319

Around you the muted noises of the village begin to subside, and the whirrs and chirrups of the river insects take over. As time wears on, you notice that a faint buzzing is growing louder. Soon the nearby insects' sounds are drowned out by this unnatural rasping. You hear the screams of frightened villagers, and the moon is blotted out by the source of the terrible buzzing – directly above your hut! You run to the door, but it will not budge. You turn back to the hut in time to see a serpentine shape sliding down through the smoke-hole. Turn to **86**.

320

You take out the locket and tell how it was entrusted to you by Ramedes before he was slain by traitorous guards. You explain that the dead Luthaur had imprisoned Ramedes immediately after the champion's return with the relic last night. Asiah Albudur comes forward and takes the locket from you. 'This is the Fate of Rangor,' she says. 'It will tell us who is the true heir to the Barony.' Inside is a faded picture of Ramedes, painted with uncanny accuracy. Even though the picture is old and cracked, as if painted centuries ago, it depicts him exactly as he appeared when you saw him last night. Asiah's face falls. 'The heir is dead. All is lost.' You try to reassure her. 'You may have lost an heir, but you have not lost the city yet. I was entrusted with a mission, and I will see it through.' With a last bow, you turn and make your way from the palace, through the crowd which parts before you. Turn to **183**.

321

As you press on, you notice clusters of purple fungus growing on either side of the path. You have to pick your way carefully along the path to avoid disturbing them – in case they carry poisonous spores. You begin to remember tales told of southern forests in which a hapless adventurer can lose himself in a maze of shifting trackways, wandering in circles until death from hunger and exhaustion catches up with him. Ahead of you, the trail divides into two. You may take the trail which slopes downwards slightly and to the left (turn to **12**), or try the other, which leads off to the right (turn to **21**).

322

You are surrounded by a shroud of mist, on a featureless plain of crystal. Your only guides are the muffled noises which penetrate the dense white vapour. There are several distinct noises, each coming from a different direction. Do you head for the:

Moaning?	Turn to **164**
Creaking?	Turn to **237**
Whispering?	Turn to **203**

323

You race around the room like a trapped rat, before remembering the skylight above your bed. Slinging your backpack across your shoulders, you heave the linen chest at the foot of your bed on to the top of it. Coughing and spluttering, you clamber up and try to batter the small window open. Just as it comes loose, there is a roar, and the door splinters amid a huge ball of flame. The bedclothes ignite immediately around you. Your adventure ends here.

324

Even though he is almost disabled by the laughing fit which grips him, your opponent manages to draw his sword and put up a spirited defence.

SLAVE MASTER   SKILL 10   STAMINA 15

If you defeat him, turn to **302**.

325

You turn your horse back towards the huge black army. Tick off a time box. A brief ride brings you within sight of it, and you watch helplessly as it engulfs a small town in the valley below. Amid the multitude, a palanquin is borne aloft by willing hands, and above it hangs a pulsing black cloud. If you follow the army at a distance, turn to **70**. If you ride down to the palanquin, turn to **368**. If you have Jheera leaves and wish to prepare them now, turn to **11**.

326

You have run out of time. While you have been dithering about in the wilderness, Kallamehr has fallen. You have failed in your mission. You flee Allansia in shame. Your name will never be considered among those of its heroes. Your adventure ends here.

327

The guards are still very happy to relieve you of your wealth. Cross off the number of Gold Pieces you give them from your *Adventure Sheet*. Unfortunately, they still have no intention of letting you into the palace. Their smirking faces begin to irritate you immensely, so you depart, seething. Turn to **130**.

328

You hurl your sword straight at the creature. It screeches as the blade slides into it right up to the hilt, but seems little affected by the wound. A

moment later, it is upon you. You are almost dragged off your feet as it sucks hard at you, but you
steady yourself and prepare to battle it.

QUAGRANT SKILL 8 STAMINA 12

You fight at −2 to your Attack Strength because you
are fighting without your sword. If you lose an
attack to the Quagrant, it sucks you into its mouth.
From then on, you will lose 2 points of STAMINA per
Attack Round as it begins to suck the flesh off your
bones *even if* you win the attack against it. However,
you may reach out and retrieve your embedded
sword, allowing you to fight without further
penalty. If you defeat the Quagrant, turn to **64**.

329

You ride until nightfall. Although you are eager to
press on, your horse is tired, and it would be too
dangerous to continue in the darkness. You dismount and prepare for a night to be spent in the
open. Tick off a time box. If you have Sige's pomander, turn to **63**. If not, turn to **367**.

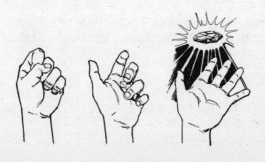

330

With a shriek, one of the circling Ectovults dives into the bowl and shatters. As it re-forms and flies off, you see that it has left behind a brilliantly polished gold shield. You watch as more Ectovults crash into the bowl, depositing other glittering treasures there. Then there is a lull. Six Crystal Warriors march over the far rim of the crater, each wielding a massive hammer. They form a circle and raise their hammers together. After five minutes they have pounded the magical relics into glowing powder; they then leave with the same clockwork precision. Soon you hear the sound of a feeble chanting approaching. If you hurry down to the middle of the bowl, turn to **228**. If you would rather stay hidden, turn to **245**.

331

In the cold light of morning you discover that you have spent the night by the side of the road. What's more, your horse is quietly grazing a short distance away. As you remount and prepare to continue, you notice a small roll of parchment tied to the pommel of your saddle. It reads:

> *Before you I stand, fair and square,*
> *Yet once you spot me I won't be there,*
> *Vanquished by a word yet kings I beat*
> *And rounded off with a rhyme so sweet.*
> *Who am I?*

Add 2 LUCK points. Tick off a time box, then turn to **7**.

332

By the time you reach the bars you are nearly exhausted (lose 1 point of STAMINA). Pausing for a brief rest, you duck down and swim back under them. Turn to **24**.

333

Rummaging among the vials and pieces of scrap paper on the desk, you come across a parchment, stained green by a sticky syrup which has spilled from a cracked bottle. You hold up the soggy sheet, straining to read the scrawl which covers it. You can't make out all the words, just occasional snippets.

> *'and do not leave the house until you are certain the danger is past . . . Under no circumstances allow . . . safe then you should make your way to your parents' village by . . . find yourself in the shifting forest you must follow the brush-bearer's gloves or be lost for ever . . .'*

If you haven't already done so, you may go to examine the puppets and cupboard (turn to **244**). Or you may continue rummaging on the desk (turn to **158**).

334

It would be too dangerous to accuse one of these powerful people outright, but there is a way by which you can *prove* the guilt of the murderer. You must insist that one of the nobles shall kiss Carolina, according to the old woman's tale. It is a strange request, but one that they will find hard to refuse – a final mark of respect for the departed ruler. The crowd are hushed, expectant. Which noble do you ask to kiss Carolina:

Dunyazad of Ikhtiyan?	Turn to 47
Madhaerios, Carolina's cousin?	Turn to 74
Sige the Silent?	Turn to 279
Asiah Albudur, the judge?	Turn to 156

335

You hurry back through the door you had entered by and find the entry-chamber full of cowled Servants of Bythos. As you enter they look up, their cavernous eyes boring into yours. You raise your sword to defend yourself, but crystal pillars erupt from the floor beneath you, trapping you like a rat in a cage. Into the chamber strides Bythos, a towering figure over fifty feet high. Turn to 313.

336

You are cold. You can't see. You thrash around with your limbs, but don't hit anything. The only sound is your own laboured breathing. Have you escaped death, or is this death's clammy chamber? You stop flailing about and rub the darkness from your eyes. As you pull your hands away, the wind is knocked out of you as bodies slam into you from all directions. Suddenly your sight returns. You are smothered in a press of desperate, hollow-eyed people. They stare at you with a mixture of pity and resignation. You struggle through them, but are brought up against thick iron bars. Beyond is a vast empty expanse of shifting colour, glimmering particles and terrifying sound. From this impossible void flashes a streak of silver. It crashes straight into the bars and shatters into a million droplets. These re-form themselves in a grotesque, leering thing which shoots off again into the distance, weaving a vaporous trail. You turn to the others, but their cold stares offer you no hope.

337

With a twist of your hips you jack-knife through the opening. Bracing your legs against the opening, you pull yourself through. Turn to **372**.

338

You catch the aged priests by surprise. Feinting to one side, you take a couple of steps and then leap, sailing high over their heads. You land nimbly, pick yourself up and race out of the Temple building. Grabbing your horse from the stables, you mount up and are soon away. Turn to **26**.

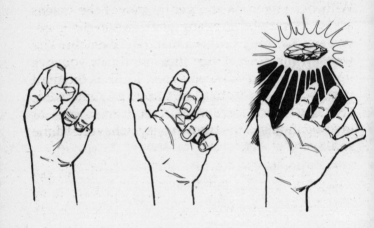

339

The chunk of crystal you are standing on starts to turn over, and you leap from it just in time. You land on the slippery crystal, unable to keep your balance. Flattened against its oily surface, you watch in horror as the black shape slams down on to the crystal a few yards away, and advances on you. Turn to **135**.

340

You lower yourself slowly down the wall until you are level with the window. Then you crane your head round to peer in. The room is dimly lit, and you strain to see the stark features of the Lady Sige, which seem to be staring back at you. You wait breathlessly for her to challenge you, and then realize that she is deep in meditation. She sits at a small table, upon which lie a board and counters. With her fingertips she gently moves the tokens across its surface. Pressing your face to the glass, you see that the board is a map of Kallamehr. You wait a while to see if Sige stirs, but finally you give up and return to the keep's roof. If this is the third window you have looked in, turn to **25**. Otherwise, you may return to your quarters (turn to **151**), or investigate any of the following if you have not done so already:

The far left wall	Turn to **397**
The left centre wall	Turn to **94**
The right centre wall	Turn to **218**

341

Suddenly it dawns on you that you recognize the voice; it is that of your old blade-master, Barolo. 'I knew who it was from the start, you old scoundrel,' you reply, 'but a knife from behind is hardly your style.' He relaxes his grip and allows you to turn round. 'We all have to change our style to suit our circumstances,' he grins, and you see that there is a wooden stump in place of his left leg. He sees your pitying expression and scoffs: 'Traded the old one in with a dragon.' Barolo invites you to spend the rest of the night at his house. Turn to **375**.

342

The main door into the keep will undoubtedly be well guarded. However, by climbing a flight of stairs in the palace walls and slipping along the walkway that runs along their top, you will be able to reach its roof. Glancing round the courtyard, you notice a coil of rope hanging from a hook outside the stables, so you wrap this round you and make your way up the stairs. You keep an eye open for any sign of the guards who occasionally patrol the walkway. Roll two dice. If the result is *less than* your SKILL, turn to **71**. If the result is *greater than or equal to* your SKILL, turn to **371**.

343

You have no time to register your foe before it is upon you. You feel fetid breath, and hear a sound as of a stone rattling against a shell. The beast's shape is hazy, and it shifts as you try to focus on it. You swing your sword, but it clacks harmlessly against a carapace. Then, from nowhere, jaws spring forth at you, and you are lost.

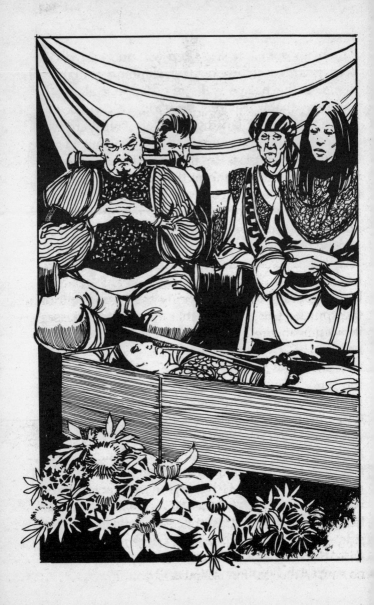

344

You take your place in the long line of citizens waiting to kiss the hand of their departed ruler. In front of you, two citizens are having a whispered argument, and you cannot help but overhear. 'I'm not having you kissin' her hand, not after you poached her finest swans!' says the wife of the pair. 'I've heard what they say! Your guilt would turn her skin black as night!' 'Hush, woman!' her husband replies. 'Always grabbing the wrong end of the spurtle. The tale goes that if a murderer kisses its victim on the lips, they'll turn black as burnt parchment. I've nothing to fear – she won't be missing her swans now, will she?' As they approach the body, they fall silent and bow their heads in reverence. Carolina lies in full regalia, the Sword of Office gripped in her right hand, while her left rests upon a cushion so that her citizens may kiss it. Your turn comes, and you find yourself looking down at the corpse of the woman who sent you on your mission. As you bend to kiss her hand you lock eyes with Luthaur, one of the heroes who remained behind to defend Kallamehr. He stands just to one side of the nobles' platform, fidgeting nervously with the pommel of his sword. Strangely, he betrays no sign of recognition. What will you do:

Mount the platform and demand
that the nobles hear your case?   **Turn to 43**

Hold up the Sealed Locket, if you
have it?   **Turn to 110**

Slip away into the crowd and watch
the rest of the ceremony?   **Turn to 159**

345

The Troll looks first at you, then at the sapling, then at you again. His brow creases with effort as he ponders your suggestion suspiciously. Finally he grunts, and begins to rip the branches from the sapling, flinging them all around. You race round after them, plucking the leaves and stuffing them in your backpack. The Troll, meanwhile, uses his much-improved tool to lever a small, spiny creature out of the hole. He snatches his prey up greedily and rams it whole into his drooling mouth. A moment later, he lets out a gurgling howl of pain. Tearing at his throat maniacally, he leaps up and down. Then he catches sight of you again. 'You trick me!' he croaks, and leaps to the attack.

TROLL   SKILL 7   STAMINA 9

If you wish, you may *Escape* after one Attack Round – turn to **248**. If you defeat the Troll, turn to **60**.

346

You race up to the rim of the bowl, then chance a look back. The Crystal Warriors are no longer interested in you. They are pounding at the magical treasures, sending up plumes of golden powder. Then, abruptly, they stop and march off. Soon you hear the sound of feeble chanting approaching. If you hurry down into the bowl once more, turn to **228**. If you wait to see what happens, turn to **245**.

347

The remaining villagers flee before you, and you ride off into the night. When you are a safe distance away, you stop and dismount. As you light your fire for the night, you wonder whether you were right to slaughter the superstitious peasants. Perhaps the prophecy was right after all, and you should have stayed to save them? Next morning, you set off once more. The land through which you are travelling starts to climb once more. Tick off a time box and turn to **7**.

348

In an instant you are on your feet, brandishing your sword. You leap at the fire and launch a mighty kick at it. Fiery embers cascade on to the stunned figures of three Black Elves, and they yelp in pain. You prepare to do battle with them, but it seems they have had enough. They lope off into the darkness. Turn to **163**.

349

The knocking sound is coming from a large stone building which has a sign outside: 'Strangecan's Wine Emporium'. Cautiously, you open the door and enter, stepping carefully over broken bottles. The shop is wrecked from top to bottom, and the floor is puddled with spilled wine. A slow, regular thumping is coming from behind the counter. Peering over it, you see a trapdoor set into the floor. A cask is wedged between the counter and the wall, preventing the trapdoor from being opened. If you try to open the trapdoor, turn to **59**. If you leave the shop and look in the other buildings, turn to **128**.

350

The vision vanishes from between the woman's hands. 'At least you're honest. Still, secrets must be earned. My companion is hungry. You must go out into the shifting forest and fetch him a tasty morsel.' She points behind you, and you turn to find yourself staring at a huge serpent. Shivering involuntarily, you edge back towards the opening in the floor. The hut lowers, and you step on to the ground. 'A rat will do nicely,' the woman calls down to you, as the thin legs straighten and the hut rises once more. If you try to escape from the forest, turn to **123**. If you obey the woman and hunt for food, turn to **395**.

351

You are thrown forward on to the ground as *something* slams into your back. You catch a vague glimpse of a silvery shape as you fall, but it rapidly screeches off into the misty wastes. Lose 1 STAMINA point. Turn to **322**.

352

The jailer cackles at your misfortune. Ramedes drops from the grille above and lands heavily. You have failed him. You have failed Kallamehr.

353

You spend an unpleasant hour pacing up and down the cell, wondering what can have gone wrong. Dunyazad told you to stay at this Temple. Why should the priests be so hostile? Eventually you are released. The High Priest explains that he has spoken with Dunyazad, and you are now to go free to continue your mission. He seems loath to release you. Nevertheless you soon find yourself back in the streets of Hasrah with your possessions returned. Turn to **136**.

354

The entry-chamber is full of cowled Servants of Bythos, but with your new-found power you scatter them effortlessly. You charge out of the palace in time to see Bythos disappearing into the mist. You head in his direction as fast as you can run, following his cracked footprints in the crystal surface. Finally you catch up with him. He has just tugged a chain free from a hoop in the ground. As you watch, it drifts away upwards. Bythos turns to you with a sneer. If you attack him, turn to **196**. If you grab the chain before it floats away, turn to **266**.

355

You wake up in a cell. You cannot tell what time of day it is. The hours drag by and nobody appears at the grille. The dull ache of hunger grows, and your spirits desert you. Kallamehr is doomed.

356

The tree is gnarled with age, and is being slowly strangled by the creepers which hug it. Foxgloves grow in profusion, all drooping elegantly to the left, towards the sunlight which filters through the leafy canopy overhead. You may collect some foxgloves and store them in your pack if you wish. If you now proceed along the right-hand path, write down the number '2' on your *Adventure Sheet* and turn to **388**. If you take the left-hand path, write down the number '3' on your *Adventure Sheet* and turn to **268**.

357

No sooner have you slashed the Anemorus into a
blubbery mess than two more erupt from the water.
You prepare to do battle with them, but are beaten
to it. Three silver flying Ectovults smash into them
and you flee, to the sounds of screeching. Turn to 3.

358

You spur your mare along the back of the ridge,
desperate to reach the village in time to warn them
of their peril. If Mema is with you, turn to 35. If not,
turn to 125.

359

You hide yourself in a pile of straw as the courtyard
fills with noise. Ramedes lets out a blood-curdling
roar, quickly followed by screams from the guards
in the keep and the harsh clash of metal on metal.
Another roar goes up from Ramedes, this time
fainter. His final cry is one of pain, and a shout of
triumph arises from the guardsmen. Saddened by
the defeat of Kallamehr's brave champion, you examine the trophy which he entrusted to you, and for
which he lost his life. Turn to 293.

360

You smash the javelin aside, and the cowled figure
gasps. He reaches down for another piece of crystal.
You must act quickly. If you know the Spitting
Fly and wish to use it, turn to 190. If you try to
charge him before he looses another missile, turn
to 257.

361

By the time you have found your weapon and groped your way back to the window, the flying apparition has disappeared. The smoke is thick now, and you can feel the heat of the floor through the soles of your boots. Will you:

Run for the door?	Turn to 61
Climb out of the window?	Turn to 304
Look for another way out?	Turn to 323

362

You set out, treading carefully, down the passage until finally you arrive at a fierce wall of fire which fully blocks it. If you go back to the river and investigate the bars, turn to 277. If you dive through the flames, turn to 157.

363

The passage is very dark, and after a few yards you nearly tumble down a steep flight of stairs. After a tortuous descent the passage widens out, and you see the warm glow of torchlight ahead. You make your way past a row of empty cells into a rough-hewn cavern, full of shadowed niches and alcoves. Your attention is drawn to the large metal grille set into the floor. At its centre is a trapdoor of thinner bars. A few feet from them, you make out a pair of hands gripping the grille tightly. Stepping closer, you see that a man is hanging from the grille, while below him a huge shape moves in the darkness, making foul sucking and gurgling noises. If you have a crossbow and wish to shoot the creature which lurks below, turn to **51**. If you leave the chamber, turn to **126**. If you rush to open the trapdoor, turn to **162**.

364

Roll two dice. If the result is *less than* your SKILL, turn to **338**. If the result is *greater than or equal to* your SKILL, turn to **220**.

365

With a mighty heave, you push over the goblet. It shatters, and its sticky contents ooze over the floor. You take the opportunity to examine the chamber. It is bare crystal, with only two exits – the door you entered by and another within a huge crystal arch. As you stare at this, you hear thunderous footsteps approaching. It must be the Master! If you wait for him to arrive, turn to **68**. If you flee through the door you entered by, turn to **335**.

366

You are beginning to lose all hope of ever finding your way out of this shifting maze of pathways when the trees ahead thin out and the trail leads into a large clearing. Add 1 LUCK point and tick off a time box. Before you is one of the strangest dwelling-places you have seen: a crude mud hut sitting proudly on four spindly legs, twenty feet off the ground. There are windows in its walls, but they are too high up for you to see inside. There is no sign of a door, even though you walk all the way round the hut. If you walk under the hut, turn to **254**. If you try to climb its legs, turn to **202**. If you wait to see what happens, turn to **145**.

367

You light a small fire, then sink into a troubled sleep. You dream of a leering face, floating gracefully in the air amid swirling clouds and cackling laughter. A huge shape looms up above you, and you wake up with a start. A curved sword is poised high above your head. You have a split second to react before it falls! *Test your Luck*. If you are Lucky, turn to **46**. If you are Unlucky, turn to **232**.

368

You spur your horse down towards the horde, trying to quell your rising fears. It is vast, and a foul stench wafts from it. As you near the bottom of the slope, you pass a dark cave entrance. Then you approach the horde. They take no notice of you, but the dark cloud above the palanquin begins to move in your direction, picking up speed. If you have a Jheera torch prepared, turn to **138**. Otherwise, turn to **113**.

369

The murky potion slides reluctantly down your throat. It doesn't taste of anything but rust and it doesn't have any noticeable effect on your body. Disappointed, you turn arou–

. . . You are lying in a heap on the ground, still clutching the empty vial. You climb groggily to your feet, and sway as a wave of dizziness sweeps over you. Angrily you hurl the vial to the ground. Tick off two time boxes and return to the paragraph you left.

370
The remaining Kokomokoa are stripping the corpses of the dead Murkurons, so you seize the chance to charge through the door, slamming and bolting it behind you. You find yourself in a small tunnel; you have to stoop to make your way along it. On either side are alcoves, muddy and rank. Ignoring these, you continue down the tunnel until it opens into a large round chamber. Turn to **82**.

371
As you sneak up the flight of stairs, you see a guardsman coming along the walkway in your direction. You flatten yourself against the wall, but it is too late. The guard peers down at you and levels his crossbow at you. 'What's your game, then?' he demands. He stands, feet astride, at the top of the flight of stairs, fifteen feet from you. If you wish to rush him, turn to **117**. If you try to talk your way out of this, turn to **198**. If you know the Spitting Fly and wish to use it, turn to **298**.

372

Inside the hut there is none of the clutter you have come to expect from the dwelling-places of magical folk. There is no furniture of any kind, no books or scrolls, not even a single vial of potion! Through the windows set in the smooth walls you can look out into the forest. Squatting in the middle of the floor is an old woman dressed in a rough shift. Her hands are raised above her head, and between them you see a shimmering vision, floating in the air. In a swirling void hangs a wall of cells, full of dishevelled prisoners. She looks you in the eyes and speaks: 'A vision from your future, perhaps? Look closely. Look hard at the slaves of the abyss! Their souls are in thrall to its Master, and you must rescue them before it is too late. This much I will tell you. If you wish for more you must pay for it. Can you speak my name?' Do you say:

'Enthymesis'?	Turn to **50**
'Aletheia'?	Turn to **80**
'Albudur'?	Turn to **101**
'I cannot'?	Turn to **350**

373

Brushing the flailing branches aside, you race in pursuit of the black figure. With a mighty effort, you smash through a wall of undergrowth. *Test your Luck*. If you are Lucky, turn to **38**. If you are Unlucky, turn to **100**.

374

Bythos snatches up the goblet and greedily drains its contents. Then he turns to you. 'Don't leave yet, *Gatherer*!' he says, smiling. 'Someone has unfinished business with you.' You try to draw your sword, but as your hand alights on the hilt an arm snakes round your neck and holds a crystal dagger to your throat. 'You may have killed me once,' Sige whispers in your ear, 'but I will have the last laugh.' Your adventure ends here.

375

Barolo directs you to a flea-ridden bunk. You collapse into it gratefully. If you have Sige's pomander and wish to wear it, turn to **33**. Otherwise, turn to **317**.

376

The locket snaps open very easily this time, and the guards shrink away from you. The nobles stare at the interior of the treasure with a mixture of bewilderment and shock. You turn the locket round in your hand and take a look within: inside is a faded picture of Ramedes, painted with uncanny accuracy. Even though the picture is old and cracked, as if painted centuries ago, it depicts him exactly as he appeared when you saw him last night. Asiah Albudur leaps to her feet and gestures for silence. 'The Fate of Rangor has decreed the truth. Ramedes is the new Baron of Kallamehr!' You clear your throat to attract her attention, then tell her of Ramedes's death. You point at Luthaur and accuse him of being a traitor. Guards surround him and he is dragged away, protesting his innocence all the while, you turn to the four nobles. Turn to **334**.

377

Leaving the glittering treasures where they lie, you drag yourself past the bars and make for the surface, lungs bursting. Just in time, you break the surface

gn/ gfhg googg

and take a deep breath. Then you strike out once more. You swim into the darkness, becoming aware of a roaring sound coming from ahead. If you swim back to the barred arch, turn to **332**. If you carry on, turn to **215**.

378

As the Quagrant lumbers in your direction, you draw Mema's blow-pipe from your pocket and point the slender tube at the creature. It begins to suck at you, and you struggle to keep your footing. At the last possible moment, you blow hard down the tube. A cloud of fine powder billows forth and is instantly sucked into the creature's gaping mouth. With a convulsive shudder it collapses backwards, choking and wheezing asthmatically. Seizing your opportunity, you draw your sword and leap in to attack.

QUAGRANT   SKILL 6   STAMINA 8

If you lose an attack to the Quagrant, it sucks you into its mouth. From then on, you will lose 2 points of STAMINA per Attack Round as it begins to suck the flesh off your bones *even if* you win the attack against it. If you defeat the Quagrant, turn to **64**.

379

Your possessions are thoroughly gone through, but the priests are not satisfied. 'What have you done with it?' demands the High Priest. You protest your innocence and explain that you are on an important mission. When you mention that it was Dunyazad of Ikhtiyan who told you to stay at the Temple, the High Priest sits up. 'We will test the truth of your story,' he says. You are led away to a cell by two of the priests. Turn to **353**.

380

Your blast catches Bythos unawares. He stumbles back in surprise, as crystals form all over him. They penetrate into him and spread throughout his body rapidly as he turns to a statue of solid crystal. Still holding the chain, you kick your opponent contemptuously. Turn to **108**.

381

There is a faint path which follows the river-bank, and you make your way along it. After a short while it plunges back into the forest. If you have three numbers written on your *Adventure Sheet*, turn to the paragraph whose number is given by the three digits. Otherwise, if you have the number '2' on your *Adventure Sheet*, add the number '3' and turn to **268**. If you have the number '3', then add '2' and turn to **388**.

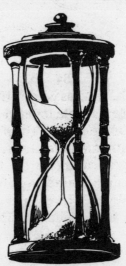

382

With a great effort you lower your head and slip off the pomander. You see it fall to the ground, then a wave of exhaustion sweeps over you and you sprawl unconscious on the bed. Tick off a time box and turn to **28**.

383

The pressure of the sand as you are dragged down is almost unbearable. Unable to move, you await the inevitable. Just as you have given up hope, you burst into space and plummet down through air full of glittering sand and treasures. Below you are swirling mists, and around you thunder booms from the starry wastes. Have you escaped death by crushing, only to be dashed against the ground below? Your speed increases, and you lose consciousness. You wake in a heap on a smooth, cold surface. Around you, magical treasures of various shapes and sizes float gently to the ground. A thick mist swirls, obscuring all but your immediate surroundings, and strange shapes shift among it. If you have Sige's pomander and know what to do with it, turn to **8**. If you examine the items, turn to **87**. If you try to find your way through the mist, turn to **116**.

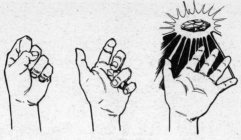

384

As Sige falls dead at your feet, a deep rumbling noise reaches your ears. It grows louder and louder until your whole body is shaking. The terrified citizens cower away. Then there is the sound of a thunderclap which almost knocks you off your feet; a smoky black tentacle curls from Sige's mouth and forms into a gaseous parody of her earthly form. It shoots straight at your face and you try desperately to ward it off with your arms. Something brittle shatters against your left hand, and the gaseous form disperses. Then pain shoots up your arm. Prepared for the worst, you look down at your left hand which is writhing within a blue vapour. You thrust it under your arm to quench the fell flame. The pain eases slightly, and you withdraw your hand. It is now shrouded in green light; as you watch, the colour changes through yellow and orange to red. The pain settles to a dull ache. The crisis over, the remaining nobles look to you for leadership. You arrange for all of Sige's servants in the city to be put under guard, and you see to the preparation of defences for the city. The other heroes, you discover, were all mysteriously slain –

presumably through Sige's villainy – so you are forced to leave the job in the hands of the remaining loyal guards. Then you prepare to journey forth once more. The hostile army still threatens, and you have a duty to Lady Carolina to fulfil. Turn to **183**.

385

Presently a villager returns and whispers briefly to one of your hosts. Without a word being spoken in your direction, he rises and gestures to the others. They all bow politely to you, then file out of the hut, closing the door behind them. You make to follow them, but find the door barred. You are imprisoned! A scratchy voice filters through to you from outside: 'Welcome, Protector. As foretold, you have come to save us from the creeping plague! Eat and rest; prepare yourself for the trial which awaits you.' Tricked by peasants! You wonder what 'creeping plague' awaits you; judging by the pitiful state of the village, it's probably lice in their sheep . . . Through the smoke-hole in the ceiling the moonlight streams into the hut. Turn to **319**.

386

You spur your panic-stricken horse back up the narrow hill path as the cloud of black hornets swirls towards you. You have pushed your mare too hard, though. She stumbles and then, as the first hornet stings her, she rears, dashing you against a jagged rock. The useless Jheera torch slips from your grasp. You hardly feel the stings of the hornets as they swarm over you . . .

387

The guards are very happy to accept your Gold Pieces. Cross off the number you give from your *Adventure Sheet*. If you gave the guards fewer than 6 Gold Pieces, turn to **30**. If you gave them 6 or more Gold Pieces, turn to **185**.

388

You push your way carefully along the narrow path. After a short while you begin to hear sounds coming from ahead. Treading carefully, you press on, expecting the worst. Suddenly you hear a loud crashing noise followed by a shrill 'By Ugbar's fingers!' This cursing is stifled by a loud 'Shush!' but other voices cry out: 'Shall I shoot 'im now?' 'Not until I give the signal!' 'What's the signal again?'

Suddenly a voice shouts 'Now!' There is a twanging sound from the trees near by and a small bow shoots from them, landing at your feet. At the same time a short, stocky figure leaps on to the path ahead of you, pointing a crossbow at you. 'Aha!' he yells, and lets fly a bolt. Turn to **189**.

389

'Most kind!' says Bythos, reaching out to take the Golden Fist. He tosses it over his shoulder, then draws in a deep breath. Before you can act, a freezing blast strikes you, and crystals form with startling speed on your skin. As Bythos continues to breathe at you, the crystals spread; soon you are encased, a living statue, doomed to live out the rest of your life as a morbid ornament for the Master of the Abyss.

390

You are rapidly surrounded by priests carrying short staves. There is something very odd about their movements – they are well trained in the fighting arts, yet move jerkily, as if under some restriction. You are encircled by a ring of staves. Will you:

Draw your sword and attempt to fight your way out?	Turn to 41
Try to leap over the priests' arms and escape?	Turn to 364
Surrender to them?	Turn to 56

391

By letting your right shoulder drop, you manage to twist your body out of the creature's grip and punch with your left fist. You scramble to your feet and stumble towards the steps, knowing that flight is your only hope. Fear lends you strength, and you race up the steps and through the trapdoor before your pursuer can lay a hand on you. Hastily, you wedge the cask back over the trapdoor to prevent the creature escaping. As you lurch out of the shop, the slow, relentless pounding begins once more. Turn to **128**.

392

The skylight! You sling your backpack across your shoulder and heave the linen chest up on to the bed, then climb on top to reach the small window. It is hard to move, and the heat is almost unbearable as you finally push it open. You pull yourself through with a grunt just as the door collapses in a welter of sparks and the room is enveloped in fire. No sooner have you found your feet on the sloping roof than you hear a loud buzzing above your head. You turn

– in time to ward off a blow from the large black creature that swoops down on you, but you stumble and lose your footing. You slide down the roof, then dangle for a moment from the guttering before dropping all the way to the ground. Roll one die and lose this number of STAMINA points. Turn to 111.

393

One moment you are reeling from the impact of something slamming into your back; the next you are floating up into the air, rapidly gathering speed. The air around you is a whirl of dancing silver shapes, and you realize that you are encased in the quivering body of a strange flying creature – an Ectovult. The ground is obscured by a carpet of shifting mist, but to your left you can see a floating wall of cells, stretching off towards the horizon. Then you plummet back down through the clouds. Turn to 36.

394

It's a good thing you changed your horse, for it means you can travel at a gallop back to Kallamehr.

You ride through the night towards the familiar beacon of the Rangor Tower. Just before you reach the city, you are overtaken by another rider. Mounted on a powerful black stallion, he is obscured by a billowing black cloak. He thunders through the city gates well ahead of you. Dawn is breaking as you enter the city and hurry to deliver your tidings to a bleary Dunyazad. Composing herself, she tries to salvage something from her shattered plans. 'Khasseeb has just come from the army. He knows the land's many ways. It would be better if he were to fetch aid. You must take on the task of your fallen comrade: scout out the invaders. Learn their ways and plans. Go now and choose a new horse; then scout east. Too much time has been lost already.' Tick off a time box and turn to **140**.

395

You wander the forest dejectedly, hunting for rodents. *Test your Luck*. If you are Lucky, turn to **176**. If you are Unlucky, turn to **243**.

396

You leap up on to your horse's back, then hoist Mema up in front of you. Soon you are galloping back along the road which brought you here. You turn off the road leading back to Kallamehr and race along a narrow track which winds up the hillside. You can see the lands far about, and off to your left a lazy plume of smoke drifts into the sky from Mema's village. Tick off a time box, then turn to **95**.

397

You lower yourself slowly down the wall until you are level with the window. Then you crane your head round to peer in. A lantern illuminates an opulently furnished room. You see nothing suspicious, however, and are about to pull yourself back up, when there is a knock at the door. From under the huge bed crawls the quaking, blubbery form of Madhaerios, dressed in a night-gown. He opens the door a crack and peers out. A tray piled high with food is passed to him, then he quickly slams and bars the door again. He turns to the tray and greedily rips a leg off a chicken. As he raises it to his mouth he pauses, then stares suspiciously at it. His eyes dart about the room anxiously, then he flings the food from him and sits back on the bed, shooting glances around the room, his nose twitching constantly. You haul yourself back up to the roof. If this is the third window you have looked in, turn to **25**. Otherwise, you may return to your quarters (turn to **151**), or investigate any of the following if you have not done so already:

The left centre wall	Turn to **94**
The right centre wall	Turn to **218**
The far right wall	Turn to **340**

398

The Crystal Warrior shatters, but you are now surrounded by the remaining five. As one, they close in and raise their hammers . . . to them you are just another trinket to be crushed.

399

You face half a dozen guards. For all your skills as a warrior, you cannot defeat six trained men at one time. You shrink back before the combined assault of the guards, only to be shoved back at them by the hostile, jeering crowd behind you. Death comes quickly.

400

While searching through the palace you have inherited, you come upon a scrying mirror, set into a wall of crystal. A Servant shuffles forward and shows you how to use it; you train it on Kallamehr, hoping to see the fruits of your sacrifice. Sure enough, the fields are full of villagers once more and the land is rejoicing under its new Baron Madhaerios. You look with pride upon a land which is freed from Bythos's clammy grip and Sige's nefarious scheming. Feeling that your sacrifice is bearable, you leave the mirror and make your way to one of the towers of the palace. As you gaze out at the vast swirling plains of the Abyss, you hear the sound of a thousand leathery wings. Soon the air is thick with circling Ectovults. For a moment you are gripped by fear; is this some last trick of Bythos? But they have only come to salute their new Ruler. Then something coils round your legs, pulling you off balance. You crash to the ground and find yourself face-to-grinning-face with Caduceus the Serpent. 'Much wisdom is mine,' he says, 'and I have much time to share it with you. I hope you will find me an entertaining companion.' Given a choice, you might have preferred lighter company; but you soon find that the serpent is as wise as he claims. With his great knowledge to guide you, you uncover secrets beyond your imagination. Your power grows ever greater, until the memory of your former life in Allansia becomes a distant dream. Finally, you unravel the mystery of travel between the planes, and embark upon an adventure which spans the cosmos and concerns the gods themselves. But that is another tale, to be found in the books of myth and legend . . .